Finding
Your Soul Family

FINDING YOUR SOUL FAMILY

A guide to personal development

Alison Wem

First published in 2018 by Alison Wem

Printed and distributed by Alison Wem Publishing
London, UK

Visit Alison Wem's website at www.yoursoulfamily.com

A catalogue record for this book is available from the British Library.

ISBN: 978-1-9997014-3-7
ISBN: 978-1-9997014-2-0 (ebook)

Edited by Steven Hiatt
Cover design by Jessica Bell

Names have been changed to protect the identity and privacy of those involved.

To my best friend, who was the catalyst for starting this journey of personal development and growth.

Contents

List of Figures

Foreword

This book can help to unravel the experiences and challenges we all face as a result of being born into our different families, which I believe were deliberately chosen by us before entering the physical world again. The purpose of our physical lives is of course to experience love in its many aspects, giving us the opportunity to grow as human beings. In this respect, we are all the same, but our journeys through life are all different and unique. Should we choose to grow from our experiences, then wonderful opportunities arise automatically for our evolution as humans. Often, experiences of a painful kind are repeated with monotonous regularity, bringing us to the point where we decide to 'grow up' properly – and this book reveals in a most creative and joyful manner how this can be accomplished.

Enjoy reading about Alison's journey, from which she has greatly benefited personally, presenting and sharing with others her insights and revelations with a view to inspiring all of us to enjoy happy, satisfying and productive lives.

It has been a pleasure and privilege to accompany Alison on her journey in writing this book, which I can heartily recommend and endorse as wisdom which can only bring about healing and nourishment for our souls.

Gerrie March C.S.N.U.
International Psychic Medium and Tutor
College of Psychic Studies, London
April 2016

Part 1

Remembering Who You Are and Where You Are Going

Create your soul map back to your 'Inner You'

Chapter 1: Introduction

Have you ever asked yourself 'What should I be doing next in my life?' The desire to move forward expressed in this simple but important question can trigger a meaningful journey of self-development and growth. *Finding Your Soul Family* is a guide to personal development. This book will help you to explore the relationships in your life and to discover your Soul Family. But first, what do I mean by 'Soul Family' and 'Soul Map'?

What Are Your Soul Family and Soul Map?

A Soul Family is a group of people that can include individuals from your biological family, adopted family, in-laws, friends, colleagues, and neighbours. All of these people can provide you with challenges and therefore with opportunities to learn. They might also share moments of kindness, enabling you to practice receiving. Both kinds of situations are opportunities for personal development and growth.

In the 21st-century people lead busy lives, and often we feel that we have little space in which we can contemplate and just 'be'. Meditation helps to calm the noisy chatter of the mind and create the space to just 'be' and connect with your conscious mind, higher

Soul family members can be individuals from your biological family, adopted family, in-laws, friends, colleagues, and neighbours.

self or soul, depending on your life view. I call this your 'inner you' to encompass all of these beliefs.

Personal development is about improving your skills and strengthening your relationships at home and at work. Your Soul Family goes beyond the meditative state and puts out to the universe the question:

'What is the right thing to do next in my life?'

Creating your soul map enables you to connect with your 'inner you' and find a place of calmness where you can receive insights into your life. This connection often leads to creating more harmony in your life and facilitates your rediscovery of your personal wisdom. In this book, you are guided through exercises with clear steps to create a map that leads you back from your conscious mind to your 'inner you'. I call this picture your soul map.

Soul maps are a visual representation of you and your life. Each one is a geometric picture; an example of one is at the start of this chapter. The outer circle of the soul map represents the circle of life. You are the circle in the middle. The other circles represent people who are important in your life. You are all interacting with one another in your Soul Family. The lines between members of your family represent either a life lesson you are helping each other learn or a special relationship. Examples of Life Lessons might be learning to listen, to be patient, or to define and hold your boundaries. When the life lesson is not clear to you, often it is the presence of a special relationship that alerts you to a lesson being learnt. Examples might include a special relationship between a grandfather and a grandson where the thing in common is the same sense of humour or a love of music. Often that certain something which makes a relationship special is quite small and perhaps hard to identify but is nevertheless very important.

Creating a personal soul map strengthens the communication between you and your 'inner you'. Your 'inner you' will assist with your personal development.

Your 'inner you' will respond to your questions with wisdom, but you need to develop the skills to hear the responses. Your Soul Family guides you in developing your ability to listen to your 'inner you' to gain meaningful insights.

Your Soul Family has the added benefit of exploring who you really are and the Life Lessons you are learning. It also allows you to explore who is in your inner circle of friends and family, the relationships you have with them and the lessons they might be learning. Attaining this knowledge brings greater understanding of the challenges individuals are facing and with that knowledge more harmony within your family and close friendships.

Finding Your Soul Family **aims** to enhance your conscious awareness of yourself. Using the techniques in this new approach enables you to undertake an honest assessment of yourself in a creative and gentle manner. Through the greater awareness gained you can make positive change in your life. Many find this leads to a happier life where they feel more complete and in balance.

My belief is that anyone can attain this level of understanding. Many people already know a lot about themselves and their family but lack a framework into which they can place this knowledge. Building your own soul map through the use of *Finding Your Soul Family* techniques provides this framework and creates a holistic picture of

Finding Your Soul Family aims to enhance your conscious awareness of yourself.

What seems fantastic today will seem ordinary tomorrow.

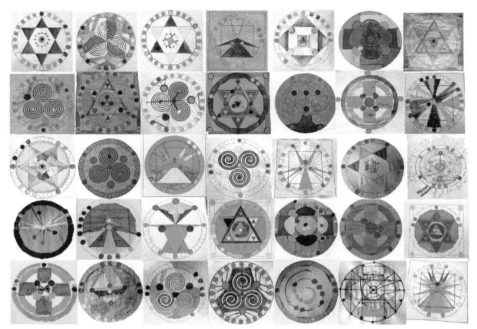

Figure 1. Student soul maps.

yourself. This in itself gives you more knowledge. It does not bring an instant realisation but more of a developing understanding over time. At some point, you will look back and realise how far you have come. What seems fantastic today will seem ordinary tomorrow.

Finding Your Soul Family is a personal development tool that helps you to find that quiet spot within yourself and to receive the wisdom you find there. All you need is the desire to do it and intuition – that feeling inside you when you know what is right for you that some people call 'gut instinct'. Using the exercises in this book, you will:

- Examine the Life Lessons and relationships in your life and use that knowledge to build a soul map, providing a holistic picture of yourself.

- **Enhance your conscious awareness of yourself** and put you back in touch with your 'inner you'.
- **Learn to use your soul map** to help your subconsciousness guide you in your personal development. It can be used in meditation to assist with hearing messages from your 'inner you'.

Let's have a look at some soul maps painted by some of my students, shown in Figure 1. They are simple yet highly personalised to the individual. Each map contains the individual, the people important in their life and their Life Lessons – and each map speaks to their maker's 'inner you'.

Soul Family pictures or soul maps are secular in nature but use geometric shapes that are found in many cultures, religions and nations. You can find them in many places, and in many contexts. Figure 2 shows some examples of such geometric designs:

Geometry is a universal language that enables you to unlock knowledge contained in your subconscious about the true nature of yourself. Often there are things about yourself that you know in a vague way, but that are not fully apparent to your conscious self. As you go through the process of creating your soul map you will gain more insight into yourself, making these things more explicit to your conscious you.

Figure 2. Manhole covers, London.

Finding Your Soul Family is a personal development tool.

Figure 3: Islamic patterns, Alcázar, Seville, showing patterns that are both finite and infinite.

The 'inner you' will connect with these pictures and bring relaxation and calmness as you colour your soul map. In working through this book you will only hear what you are ready to hear. If you do nothing else, carry the book around with you. Dip into it and read the call-out texts and look at the pictures to gain an understanding of the concepts.

I believe this is a book you will read many times. You can progress through it once and gain one level of enjoyment and understanding. If you appreciate what it has to teach, you will pick it up again at a later time and find a whole new level of meaning. This book will help you to understand who you really are, where you are going and all that you continue to be.

In that calm space within you, you will find a wisdom you did not know you possessed. So relax and enjoy the journey to rediscov-

Help you to understand who you really are, where you are going and all that you continue to be.

ering who you really are. It is my desire that by the end of this book you will know yourself, love yourself and be enjoying your life.

Hints and Tips

- In this world of high achievement, we have a tendency to approach self-improvement with great zeal. *Finding Your Soul Family* does not subscribe to this approach. Above all, the exercises in this book are to be **enjoyed and savoured.** If at any time the exercises do not feel like this, put it away and try again on another day.
- **Well-being is lined up outside your door.** You just need to allow it to come into your life. Understanding yourself is a move toward turning the handle of that door.
- **Take one simple step** to start this journey.

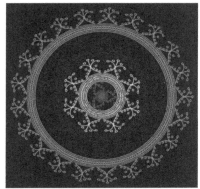

Figure 4. Mandala, a circular figure representing the universe in Hindu and Buddhist symbolism.

Delight in the richness of your life

Chapter 2: Steps for Developing Your Soul Map

When I say be creative, I don't mean that you should
all go and become great painters and poets.
I simply mean: Let your life be your painting.
Let your life be your poem.'

– Osho

From working in an art business I learnt that the universal language expressed in the form of art connects directly to our hearts and our inner selves. You do not have to be a great artist to experience the joy of creating art. Using geometric templates, you can find great joy in choosing the colours and painting the templates. The child in you will return, which enables you to connect with the 'inner you' and from there to the wider universe. Geometric shapes are important in all cultures and religions. Geometry is fundamental to science and the universe. The schools of ancient Greece, particularly that of Pythagoras, made a special study of geometry. Many of the sacred sites of the ancient world, such as the pyramids of Egypt and South America and the stone circles of Western Europe such as those at Stonehenge, Carnac and Avebury, were constructed

Art connects directly to our hearts and our inner selves.

to conform to what is known as 'Sacred Geometry'.[1] These shapes reproduced patterns upon which it is thought the world and the universe are constructed. Geometric shapes are a fundamental part of our being. This process of connecting to your 'inner you' guided by geometric shapes, creating the picture given to you by your subconscious, is available to all humans. This is what I have called Soul Art.

In creating your own soul map using Soul Art, you will explore your relationships with blood family, in-laws, adopted family, colleagues, neighbours and even strangers who for a moment play a part in your life. You will explore your inter-relationship with humanity and the Life Lessons you are learning with a prime focus on your inner circle, your Soul Family.

Building a picture of your Soul Family is like putting a jigsaw puzzle together. Analysis of your current family identifies the straight edges of the puzzle to create the frame. The challenge is to find and fit together the pieces that make up the middle to create the picture. This picture builds to show how you relate to each other to help you to understand individual family members and the lessons you are all learning. Meditation assists in gaining greater insight. Meditation is the practice of concentrated focus upon a sound, object, visualisation or breath in order to increase awareness of the present moment. It reduces stress, promotes relaxation and enhances personal and spiritual growth. Do give it a try. There are many good apps and downloads available on the market which include guided meditations to help you practice.

Meditating over your family picture will bring additional information and insight to you to guide your personal development. Like

Soul Art is painting geometric shapes to aid connection to your 'inner you'.

---

1 Detailed information on Sacred Geometry can be found in the book *How the World Is Made: The Story of Creation According to Sacred Geometry* by John Mitchell with Allan Brown.

all personal development, this happens over a period of time rather than instantly.

Overview of the Seven Steps to Creating Your Soul Map

You have already seen what a soul map looks like, but here is a quick summary of the steps you need to take to create your soul map to give you a broad overview of the process. You have already taken the biggest step, which is to find out about your 'inner you'. You are now just seven simple steps from creating your own soul map, the route back to your 'inner you'. **Find a quiet space** where you will not be disturbed when you try this for yourself. Here are the steps:

1. **Explore what you already know about yourself and your family** – capture the information.
2. **Your family structure guides the shape of your soul map.** Using the Foundation Template, place your family members in your soul map. The Foundation Template can be found in the Resource appendix, or you can download it from www.yoursoulfamily.com. You are the circle in the middle. The other circles around the rim are people who are important in your life and may be helping you with the Life Lessons you want to learn. Choose a place for each family member and write their name by the circle. Do you have an inner circle of supporters? If you do, draw some circles near you and name the individuals.
3. **Decide on the colours of your individual family members.** Each person is speaking to you from one of the chakra colours – red, orange, yellow, green, blue, indigo or mauve. We have some exercises to help you decide which colour they are using. Also think about the colour that would represent you the best.

4. **Family dynamics guide the core design of your soul map.** Decide on the shape of the central part of your soul map which is right for you and your family. You have two choices:

    - Choose a template that pleases you most from the selection provided in this book. Then use the example in the book or go to www.yoursoulfamily.com to download and print it. It will be larger than the pictures in this book and will be the starting point for creating your own soul map. Using the positions you chose in the previous step as a guide, move your family members to your chosen template.

    - Use the Foundation Template which gives the basic structure and **design your own centre** for your soul map.

    Both approaches work well. Your choice should really depend on which one you feel most comfortable with. Many people start with a template for their first soul map so they can quickly appreciate what the technique has to offer and then go on to create their own design at a later date.

5. **Colour your soul map** with water colours, chalk, felt pens or acrylic paint. All are easy to obtain in the high street. You want the colour to be rich and vibrant, so be careful not to use too much water with the paints. I believe paints are a good colouring medium as they take more thought to use than other media. This concentration eases the busy chatter of your mind, enabling you to receive your message more easily.

6. **Before you start** to colour your soul map, ask yourself: **'What is the message that I should hear at this moment in my life?'**

Ask yourself,
'What is the message
I should hear
at this moment in
my life?'

7.   **Relax and enjoy colouring** this picture of you *for you*. Feel the calmness start to come in.

Your message will arrive in the next few days. It may come in some unexpected ways – as a knowing, a dream, a phrase on the radio echoing a thought or a picture or words on a billboard jumping out at you. Be alert so that you are able to receive your message when it chooses to arrive.

    If after a while you are unsure whether you have received your message correctly, repeat the question again while you are reflecting on your soul map. Wait to see what answer you get. If the message is the same as the original one, it is highly likely you received it correctly. This is not a process to hurry through. Take your time to receive your message. The wisdom you gain on this journey is wisdom about yourself, so it is important that you do not feel you have to rush.

    In the following chapters, you will receive more detailed guidance on how to undertake each step. There are more detailed steps for each phase of the building process, worked examples for you to follow, hints and tips, feedback from students who have attended my workshops and a case study.

    The case study follows Andrea's progress in building and using her soul map. She is a dear friend of mine and one of my earliest students, and she has kindly agreed to let me share her voyage of self-discovery using *Your Soul Family* techniques. Throughout Andrea's journey I have made notes on the exercises she undertook and the insight they brought. Much of what I share in the coming pages is an edited version of these notes.

Your message will arrive in the next few days.

The wisdom you gain on this journey is of yourself.

Meet Andrea

Andrea writes about her own journey: 'It is said that we choose our name and our parents before we are born. The meaning of my family name, Holloway, is derived from the Old English *Hol,* which means "sunken" or "hollow", and *Weg,* meaning "way" or "path". It could also mean "holy way".

'When I was researching a house we had moved into in Wokingham, Berkshire, an old resident told me that the lane near our house was originally part of a network of roads that led from the outlying farms to the centre of Wokingham, where in past times a cattle market was held. Before lorries, sheep were herded together from the fields and driven down these roads to market. To make this movement easier and to prevent individual animals from wandering off, the road was hollowed out with raised banks and hedges on either side.

'Symbolically, I feel that my chosen name is saying that my telling my story will help provide you with a guide for you to find your way from outlying areas back to the centre of your Soul Family using guided pathways, or "hollow ways", like the pathways used by our ancestors to guide their herds. There are many routes to personal development. This is but one, and I hope that my story will help you to decide if this path would be of assistance to you.

'When faced with severe challenges in my life, the only place to look for strength was within myself. When I did this, I was extremely surprised by what I saw and learnt. Initially all I was asking myself was "What is the right thing to do next in my life?" What I found from this simple process was a wealth of knowledge and wisdom gained from experiencing life.'

In this voyage of rediscovering, Andrea set out with only her intuition to guide her. Intuition is that voice or feeling inside that talks to you, often when you need to make decisions or at times of stress. Some people call it their 'gut instinct'. I like to think of it as simply asking yourself, 'Does this feel right?' Your brain can look at the positives and negatives of a situation or decision to advise you on what is the right thing to do. However, having done this analysis I now find that my inner knowing is more reliable than my brain in making the right decision for me. In this approach, I am not talking about impetuousness, but rather considered learning or decision-making through consulting the 'inner you'.

Based on observation of the twists and turns that Andrea's voyage and those of other students took, I have created some guidelines plus hints and tips you might like to use. Please remember that these are only guidelines: you need to make this journey your own, so do use only the techniques that appeal to you. Let your 'inner you' guide you on your journey.

As you work with Your Soul Family your energy becomes more open, improving the ability to talk to your 'inner you'. After working on a *Your Soul Family* exercise and before you get on with your everyday life, it is therefore advisable to 'close down' your energies. Otherwise, as you go out and about you will be very sensitive to people's emotions and thoughts. Closing down is much like when you leave your home: you would not leave the front door wide open for all to enter. After you have finished Soul Family work, close your eyes and imagine a big front door on your chest. Close the door, take a big key and lock the door. Put the key in your pocket and know that you are protected and safe.

Once it's built, you can use your soul map as a development tool and focus for the lessons you are learning. *Finding Your Soul Family* is

Andrea set out with only her intuition to guide her.

Keep a diary of key thoughts, dreams and insights to make sure you capture them.

aimed at improving your interpersonal skills, appreciating the place love and compassion have in your life, and helping you to understand the lessons you are trying to learn along with your classmates whom you are learning them with. Throughout the process it is a good idea to keep a diary of any thoughts, dreams and insights you have to ensure that valuable information is captured.

It is worth remembering as you start to do the exercises and techniques in *Finding Your Soul Family* that there is no rush. The journey is more important than the destination, so the process should be savoured and enjoyed. If at any time it feels too difficult, put your soul map away and take it out again at a later time. The answers to your queries on what is right for your soul map will come to you and you will wonder why you found it hard earlier.

Now let's look at each step of your journey in more detail.

> *The journey is more important than the destination.*

Let your work be sweet

Chapter 3: What Do You Already Know about Yourself and Your Family?

Before you design your soul map, you need to do some work to reflect on and write down what you already know about yourself and your family and friends. This should not be a long story but key facts, your life events, who is important to you and who they relate to most easily and who they find a challenge. When you think about yourself and your family in a quiet and calm space you will be amazed at all the things that you implicitly know but have never articulated before.

The objective of this phase is:
- To collect as much information as you know today about yourself and the people who are important to you in your life – who the individuals are, their key relationships and potential Life Lessons any of you may be learning.

We will now go through a couple of exercises to help you to access the information you already know.

Your Current Life Review
Everybody's life has its ups and downs. The aim of this exercise is to observe your past and identify the highs and lows to gain insight.

Observe your past and identify the highs and lows to gain insight.

19

Reflecting on your life so far, you will be able to gain insight on who you are and where your life is going. Observation will highlight if there are:

- common causes for the ups and downs,
- repeated challenges.

Repeated challenges are an indication of a life lesson, such as listening to people or maybe speaking up for yourself, needing to be learnt.

Whoever accompanies you through the ups and downs of your life are potential candidates for being part of your Soul Family. Your Soul Family can consist of blood family, adopted family, in-laws, friends, colleagues and neighbours. They are the important people in your life.

Observation of your life will also confirm what you have learnt so far. You will start to appreciate changes you might want to make for the next stage in your life.

In this exercise you will practise being a 'detached observer'. Students are often surprised by what they learn about themselves by being the 'detached observer'. You are much more objective about your life than when you are living the moment. With that objectivity comes insight.

The second part of this exercise will ask you to group your observations into positive behaviours and areas for improvement. This often brings fresh insight.

S-Curve of Personal Development

Life is never static. Relationships, personal success or challenges are dynamic and constantly changing. However, there is a typical cycle to change and is represented by the S-curve model.

Become the
detached observer
of your life.

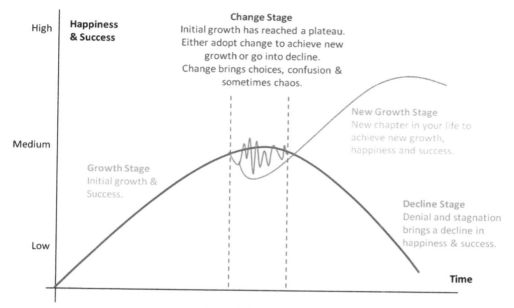

Figure 5. S-curve model.

The model represents your life over time. There will be periods where you are in growth and then you begin to plateau. Once you reach a plateau you will need to make change to move into growth again. If you do not do something different you will drift into decline.

Change is not always easy. You may be deciding what it is you want in a new chapter of your life. This brings choices you will need to consider and make. Your change might be about how you run your life, time you give yourself for personal relaxation and development or perhaps the balance between your work and your home life.

Change comes in many guises. As it brings you into unfamiliar ground you might feel discomfort in the early part of the change which reduces your feeling of happiness. You will get used to the

Change is not always easy.

change with perseverance and be able to achieve new growth and greater feelings of completeness and happiness.

Over time your life will probably be a series of S-curves. The new growth will eventually reach a plateau and you will need to consider what you would like to do next to achieve your next level of growth. By looking at your life you can decide where you are in the S-curve as an indicator of what you should be doing next – keep going or making changes to achieve new growth. In the context of Your Soul Family the changes are likely to be about relationships with members of your soul family and the Life Lessons you are all trying to learn.

It is my belief that just understanding how life works helps you to engage with it to achieve the maximum personal development. Challenges presented to you are opportunities to learn Life Lessons. Often by appreciating that fact, you approach the challenge in a more positive frame of mind seeking to get the greatest learning, rather than feeling you are the victim of a situation.

Relationships are often a challenge as they ask you to stretch to your greatest potential – for example, to be a good husband or father. The more you understand about yourself, the more you are able to appreciate the good behaviours you have acquired and perhaps the ones you need to improve.

You are now going to take a look at your life to date to see what you know about yourself and to discover the changes you might like to make.

Review Your Current Life

Understanding what has occurred in your life so far and whether it made you feel good or bad can help to inform the changes you might like to make going forwards.

Decide where you are in the S-curve as an indicator of what you should be doing next.

Start to appreciate changes you might want to make.

You are now going to plot your life events to date. Use the blank chart in the Resources appendix or download our workbook which contains the chart and others to help you to design and create your soul map. Andrea has agreed to share her life chart. Her example will help you to understand what I am asking you to try. Give it a try and see what it reveals. You may be surprised at how much you remember. If as you remember some of the low events you start to re-experience the pain of the event, take a mental step backwards and say to yourself, 'I am only remembering this past event, not living it'. This should ease the pain.

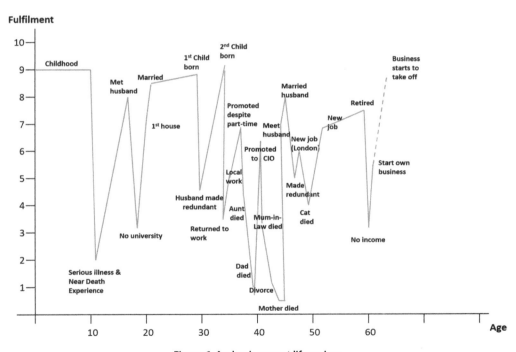

Figure 6. Andrea's current life review.

How did you find it? Doing this exercise can help you to be more objective about the events in your life. For the key high and low events, try to take a step back and be the 'detached observer'. Ask yourself:

Peaks and troughs in your life are often life events with people you love.

- What did I learn from this event?
- Would I do anything different if I was doing this a second time?

Note your answers. Do not be surprised if your peaks and troughs are mainly about key events with people you love – meeting a lover, committing to a partner, birth of a child, loss of a loved one. Work events are often in the middle band. All of this is quite common.

Gaining Insight from Your Current Life Review

Using the facts about your life – life events, emotions, learnings and participants from the previous exercise, now you will assess your personal strengths. You can use these to move your life forward. You will include the key people and Life Lessons in your soul map which is a visualisation of you and your life.

Identify areas you may want to deal with to improve the next stage of your life.

Likewise, you will also identify areas that you may want to deal with to improve the next stage of your life. Through this exercise you will step into becoming the 'detached observer' of your life to help you gain greater insight.

There is a chart to help you to capture your insights in a more structured manner. There is one in the Resources appendix but you could also download our workbook with this chart and others to help you design and create your soul map. Figure 7 shows Andrea's Life Observation chart. It might help you to understand what you need to do. We will then go through some detailed steps to guide you in creating the chart.

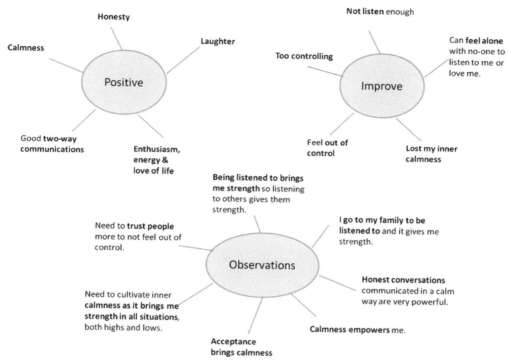

Figure 7. Andrea's life observation chart.

Strengths

Look back at your life review and remember the times when you felt joy and life felt successful. Ask yourself these questions and note your response.

1. What special skills did you display at those times?
2. What are the most valuable habits and behaviours do you have?
3. What do most people admire about you?
4. What are your most valuable behaviours?

Look at your answers and summarise what are your three main strengths.

Areas to improve

Remember the darker times in your life when things have gone wrong and you did not feel happy. Now ask yourself these questions and note your response.

1. What old weaknesses or negative patterns are most closely associated with these difficult times?
2. What are the negative or destructive trends in your behaviour that causes pain to others or yourself?
3. Sometimes certain traits or behaviours of others can awaken a negative response in you. What traps do you tend to fall into? What are your 'hot buttons'?
4. What are you most afraid of?

Look at your answers and sum up what are your three main areas for improvement.

Reflection and observations

You are now going to look back over the exercise you have just done and note the insights you have gained into yourself. Try to be the detached observer and be objective about your life to date. Answering these questions may assist you:

- What is the impact of both the positive and negative behaviours on your life events?
- What did you learn from this exercise?
- Note your observations.

Look at your areas for improvements and ask yourself if you have recognised these as Life Lessons you need to learn. Is someone

Try to be the detached observer and be objective about your life to date.

in your life helping you to learn any of these Life Lessons? They could be operating with you as a supporter or a challenger. These are important facts about your life which you will want to include in your soul map.

In the next exercise we will capture the detail of the
- Important people in your life
- Life Lessons you have learnt or are learning
- Special relationships you are experiencing to help you with learning.

You will consider who may be creating challenges for you to help you learn these lessons or who is guiding you in practising them.

If you have already created a soul map, consider the insight you have gained into yourself through the exercise you have just done. Consider if it is new insight and if so how you might want to include it in your soul map.

- Does the insight from this exercise introduce any new soul family members? Where would you place them in your soul map and what colour do you feel the new people are?
- Add the new lesson/relationship lines to your soul map design and if there are any, the new family members.

Do these changes alter the dynamics of your soul map making you want to move people around or change colours or even construct a new soul map? If the answer is yes, make the changes but do not forget to consult with your 'inner you'. If you need the Your Soul Family templates to help create a new soul map, they are in the Resources appendix or you can download a copy from www. yoursoulfamily.com.

Life is a journey of self discovery taken one step at a time.

If **you have yet to create your first soul map,** we will lead you through the steps you need to take in the following chapters.

Hints and Tips

- Analysing your life to date can help to improve how you behave in the future.
- By looking at yourself and making observations in the third person, you'll find that you are much more objective and insightful.

Collate and Capture Your Life Facts

In the previous exercise you will have started to reflect on your life, who is accompanying you and some skills you may have learnt or are learning. Now we want to capture this information and if possible expand on it. This exercise is worthwhile even if you have already created a soul map. It will capture the fundamental information about you and your soul family so the detail does not get lost. It would be such a shame to forget the insight you have worked so hard to gain. Everyone's memory can mislay important details over time.

The previous exercise gives you the basic facts of your life. It is sufficient to create a meaningful soul map. However, the next exercise will enhance your life facts and help you to create a richer soul map.

Now is the time to reflect on and write down what you already know about your family and friends. You can use the previous exercise to get you started. This should not be a long story but key facts about individuals, who they relate to most easily and who they find a challenge. Thinking about your family in a quiet and calm space

Now is the time to reflect on and write down what you know about your family and friends.

you will be amazed at all the things that you implicitly know but have never articulated before.

- **The aim of this exercise is to capture what you know** about you and your soul family in a structured manner. As you gain more insight into yourself and your life over time, I would advise that you update the information here so you have a point of reference for the facts of your life which you are going to visualise in a picture which is your soul map.

Capture what you know about your soul family in a structured manner.

Just to remind you, a life lesson is about learning a skill which helps you to run your life more easily. Examples might be learning to; listen to others, hold your boundaries or love unconditionally. Life Lessons being learnt are key facts about your soul family.

Family Information Tables

To help you with this activity we have developed two tables for you to put your information into. Let's take an overview look at these tables before we look at the detailed steps to create them. The first one, shown in Figure 8, captures your Life Lessons. The second one, shown in Figure 10, captures Life Lessons being learnt between family members. Let me talk you through them.

Name of key person in your life (a soul family member)	Your Life Lesson the key person is helping you with	Life Lesson you are helping the key person with	Special Relationship between you if a Life Lesson cannot be identified

Figure 8. Family Information Table – your Life Lessons (extract)

Figure 8 shows an extract of the first table, which focuses on you. It captures those you have a key relationship with and the Life Lessons they might be helping you learn. A full-sized table is available in the Resources appendix.

In the **first column,** record the name of an important person in your life. It is not always the person you get on with the best. It can be a person who challenges you to practise a lesson which can sometimes be hard for you. In **column 2,** add a life lesson you think that this person may be helping you learn. A life lesson might be learning to listen or learning not to always say yes.

Relationships flow both ways, so in **column 3** you can record if there is a life lesson that you may be helping the person in column 1 with. There may not always be a reciprocal lesson. If you are not sure what the Life Lessons are in columns 2 and 3 but you are aware that you have a special relationship with the person in column 1, do not put anything in column 2 or 3 but note the relationship in **column 4.** In column 4, note the basis of this special relationship. It might be a shared love of gardening or same sense of humour.

Name of key person in your life (a soul family member)	Your Life Lesson the key person is helping you with	Life Lesson you are helping the key person with	Special Relationship between you if a Life Lesson cannot be identified
Huband	Rebalancing lost love		
Daughter	Patience	Being organised	
Dad	Speaking up for myself	Being in touch with their own knowing	Gardening
Mum	Seeing the other person's viewpoint		
Best friend			Companionship

Figure 9. Andrea's Family Information Table – her Life Lessons (extract)

You need to use your observation skills to help you identify what it is. An extract from Andrea's Family Information Table for her Life Lessons is shown in Figure 9.

The second Family Information Table looks at key relationships and Life Lessons between members of your Soul Family. Figure 10 shows an extract of this table. A full-sized one can be found in the Resources appendix. This time we are looking at members of your family who have an important relationship which is helping to teach them a life lesson. Record in **columns 1 and 2** the names of these people. Add the life lesson one or both of them are learning in **column 3.** If you are unable to identify the life lesson, try to identify the special relationship and record it in **column 4.**

Name of key person in your life (a soul family member)	Name of key person(s) in your life with a relationship with the column 1 person	Life Lesson being learnt	Special Relationship between these people if a Life Lesson cannot be identified

Figure 10. Family Information Table – family member Life Lessons (extract)

An example from Andrea's Family Information Table appears in Figure 11. You will see that there are a couple of relationships where the life lesson was unknown at the beginning of Andrea's journey. It was only later that Andrea found out that her dad and her son both needed to practise judgement and that they used humour to ease learning that lesson and make it easier to discuss.

Name of key person in your life (a soul family member)	Name of key person(s) in your life who has a relationship with the column 1 person	Life Lesson being learnt	Special Relationship between these people if a Life Lesson cannot be identified
Dad	Son		Same sense of humor
Daughter	Nanny	Learning to breathe deeply to help her asthma	Also have a shared love of singing to practice the breathing
Mum	Step-Mum and Aunt		Widows, so understand how each other feel
Mum	Seeing the other person's viewpoint		

Figure 11. Andrea's Family Information Table – family member Life Lessons

Detailed Steps for Completing the Family Information Tables

It might be worth using a pencil for this task and having a rubber at hand as you will probably want to change what you capture as new thoughts come to you. Let's start by looking at your life lesson table first to see what you already know about yourself and how you interact with your family and friends.

Your Life Lessons

Here are the four steps you need to undertake. The order of completing the columns is not sequentially 1 to 4, as people seem to find it easier to identify the people in column 1 before they explore the relationships. We are using the table in Figure 8.

1. List the **important people in your life** – record in column 1.
2. Identify any Life Lessons which the person in column 1 is **helping you with** – record them in column 2.
3. Identify any Life Lessons which you are **helping the person in column 1 with** – record them in column 3.

4. If you are unable to identify life lesson(s), try to identify any special relationships between you – record them in column 4.

Now let's look at each step in more detail.

1. **List the important people in your life.**
   In my experience, most people choose to list all their people in column 1 rather than filling out the table taking each person row by row. The choice is yours and you should approach the task in whichever way you find the easiest.

   When you make your list in column 1 it can be very tempting to include only the people who are currently in your life. Do also give some consideration to former partners and close friends plus grandparents who may have passed. They have played a significant role in your life, so you may have been learning some Life Lessons together.

2. **Identify any Life Lessons you think you may be learning assisted by the person(s) in column 1.**
   Look at the list in column 1 and think about why each person is important to you. Think about any Life Lessons you may be learning and write them down in column 2. For example, lessons may be improving communication or overcoming jealous love.

   Likewise, you may be helping the person in column 1 to learn a lesson. If so, record that lesson in column 3. If either you or the column 1 people are learning further Life Lessons together you will need to split this into additional rows. For yourself, think about any repeated challenges you have in your life. Is there a life lesson you need to be learning? For me, I had increasingly difficult managers and I could not understand why I kept getting them. It was my dad, who was used to working in business, who pointed out that I was not managing my boundaries and making it clear

Approach the task in whichever way you find the easiest.

what was acceptable and what was not acceptable. My dad and I did not have an easy discussion, as I thought it was my manager's problem rather than mine. Once I understood the situation and took action to manage it, my relationship with my manager improved. Finally, after having a really challenging manager to check out my skills, I have since worked with great managers. I have to say this was not an easy life lesson for me to learn!

It is not uncommon that once you have learnt a lesson, the challenges that push you to practise this lesson fade from your life.

3. Identify any special relationships.

Typically, if you are unable to identify a life lesson being learnt by either yourself or the column 1 person, you might be able to identify a special relationship. An example might be a common interest such as music or history or perhaps the same sense of humour. What makes a relationship special can be quite nebulous, so look for small things rather than big things. If you do not know why you relate to each other, just note the special relationship. Focus on what you do know rather than fret about what you do not know.

Family member Life Lessons

Now let's run through a similar exercise looking for Life Lessons between family members. This is often a rewarding exercise, as there is much you intuitively know about your family but have not given much thought. By becoming an observer, you can start to understand your family much better. We are using the table in Figure 10.

1. **Identify family members who have a significant relationship with each other** and record them in columns 1 and 2.

> *Once you have learnt your lesson, the challenges to practise it often fade from your life.*

> *For special relationships, look for the small things rather than big things.*

2. Identify any Life Lessons which are being learnt by either person in columns 1 and 2 and record these lessons in column 3.

3. Or identify any special relationships and record them in column 4.

1. Identify family members who have a significant relationship with each other.

   It is important here not to just put the column 1 person's partner. We are trying to look at relationships and lessons across traditional partnering relationships. There may be a relationship which is sometimes not an easy one, as the column 2 person could be challenging the column 1 person to change their life in some way. Think about family gatherings or times when you meet up with good friends and try to understand the dynamics that are going on in the group. In your mind, be an observer of your group and see what you find out. It is worth remembering that our greatest challengers can be our best teachers.

Our greatest challengers can be our best teachers.

2. Identify any Life Lessons which are being learnt by either person in columns 1 and 2.

   As in the previous table, you've identified a relationship between two people and are trying to identify a life lesson they may be learning and/or helping each other with. Use these lessons to explore links between people.

3. Identify any special relationships.

   If you cannot identify the life lesson, look for a special relationship. An example would be Andrea's mother, aunt and mother-in-law, who understood each other more as they were widows together. It was only much later in Andrea's journey that she found out the true depth of that special relationship and the lesson they were learning together.

Now try to complete columns 1 through 3. Remember: If you are unsure of the life lesson but know two family members are linked, see if there is a special relationship. If you cannot identify the special relationship, just note that there is one.

In doing this simple exercise, Carol was surprised at what she found out about herself. Carol had recently gone through a challenging divorce and was now living happily with her dog, Buttercup. Through doing this exercise Carol realised that in her life key people were polarised either as a supporter or a challenger, with nothing in between. She also discovered that her Soul Family members were mostly good friends. She had shifted her focus away from the traditional roles of mother, father and siblings to people of her own choosing. Carol is now looking at the challenges to determine what her Life Lessons are.

Hints and Tips

- **Be selective.** Try not to make the list exhaustive. Somewhere between twelve and twenty-four people is good.
- **Soul Family members** are not just blood family. They can also be drawn from your in-laws, adopted family, friends, neighbours and colleagues.
- **Lessons are mostly about how you interact with people or how you feel about yourself.** They may be of the nature of improving communication, defining and maintaining boundaries, or overcoming jealous love. Use these types of lessons to explore links between people. Note your conclusions.
- **Special relationships might be between a grandparent and grandchild** who might have a common interest such as music or perhaps the same sense of humour. What makes a relationship special can be quite nebulous, so look for small things rather than big things.

- **Special relationships across generations are quite common** – grandparents can have a key role to play in your life. They may not be there through all of your life, but they can have a significant impact on your learning key Life Lessons.
- **If you do not know why two family members** relate to each other, just note the special relationship.
- **Focus on what you do know** rather than fret about what you do not know.
- **Do not rush this phase.** It is an important foundation to the design of your soul map. You may find that more things come to you over time, in which case just update your table. I believe it is worth doing this exercise and then thinking about it over the following week, adding to it as information comes to you, before you go on to the next phase.
- **Remember to close down when you have finished** working on identifying your Soul Family.

You will surprise yourself with how much you have observed and how this exercise brings this knowledge into your conscious mind.

ဢ〇ဢ
Focus on what you
do know rather than
fret on what you
do not know.
ဢ〇ဢ

Look at the Bigger Picture of your life

Chapter 4: Your Family Structure Guides the Shape of Your Soul Map

The shape and nature of your picture will depend on who you are, your values, beliefs, relationships with others and the Life Lessons you are learning. Working with your 'inner you', you will build and colour the picture that appeals to you. If it pleases you, it is the right picture for you. It is a wonderful gift to yourself which will provide great insight and knowledge.

The objective of this phase is:

- To place your family members from your Family Information Tables into your soul map.

This is the start of your soul map design.

Basic Soul Map Structure

Try starting with a circle which is as round and vibrant as a juicy Spanish orange ready for harvest. Inside the circle your family members will be represented by smaller circles and the lines between them are either relationships or Life Lessons to be learnt or practised. To help you get started we have a Foundation Template. A full-size one is available in the Resources appendix or can be downloaded from www.yoursoulfamily.com.

Start with a circle as round and vibrant as a juicy Spanish orange ready for harvest.

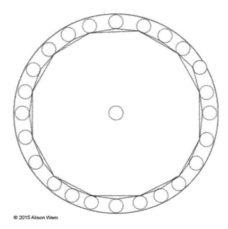

© 2015 Alison Wem

Figure 12. Foundation Template.

I find this step so exciting as it is the start of your soul map taking shape. To reiterate, the basic soul map has these characteristics:

- The large round circle represents the circle of life.
- Inside it Soul Family members are represented by smaller circles.
- You are the circle in the middle, and the family members are on the outer edge.
- Lines between members represent relationships or lessons being learnt or practised.

Family members tend to be on the outer rim of the circle. You can choose where to place individuals. The remaining space inside the circle is for you to explore. It may contain family members who make up your inner circle with whom you have a special relationship. Here is a simplified version of Andrea's placement of family members in her soul map.

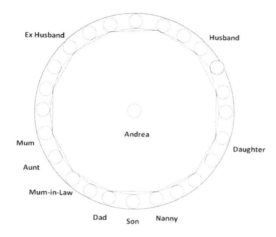

Figure 13. Andrea's simplified family placement.

Detailed Steps to Place Your Family Members in Your Soul Map

Write your name or 'Me' beside the circle in the middle. Now use the information you have observed about your family and gained from your intuition to place your family members in the picture. Just keep asking yourself, 'Does this feel right?' and follow the answer.

Here are the five steps you need to undertake to place your family members from your Family Table into your soul map:

1. Identify any inner circle of supporters.
2. Identify any grouping of family members.
3. Move the remaining family members.
4. Add relationships/lessons.
5. Review your picture.

Let's look at each step in more detail.

Keep asking yourself, 'Does this feel right?'

Your inner circle of supporters are those you turn to when all is going wrong.

1. **Identify any inner circle of supporters.**

   Do you have any special Soul Family members who are your supporters or inner circle? They are not always your life partner, so consider other supporters, like a child, friend or parent. They are the people you may turn to when all is going wrong or you need sound advice. If you have an inner group of family members, draw their circles inside the rim near your own circle and write their name by the circle.

2. **Identify any grouping of family members.**

   Look for natural groupings of family members in your Family Information Table and circle them. Typically, they are where there is more than one person in column 2 of Figure 11. In Andrea's table a grouping would be her mum, her aunt and her mother-in-law, who were widows. At this stage, the Family Information Table may not have captured all of the natural groupings in your family. Stop for a while and think about your family and consider if there are any further ones you can identify – for example, sisters who always gravitate together even if they are grown up and have their own families. If you think of some, add them to your table and then continue.

   a. Take each grouping into your soul map. **Ask your 'inner you' where each group should be placed** – at the top left, top right, bottom left or bottom right.

   b. **Remain still, wait to feel what seems right** and then place the grouping.

   That feeling is your intuition working. In Andrea's example, her widow group were in the bottom left-hand quadrant. Repeat step 2 for each group.

3. **Move the remaining family members.**
   Move the remaining family members into the circle, asking your 'inner you' where is most appropriate – at the top left, top right, bottom left or bottom right.

4. **Add relationships/lessons.**
   Add the **relationship/lesson lines between the family members** and label them.

5. **Review your picture.**
   a. **Review the result** and if by adjusting a family member's placement you can reduce the crossing of lines, please do so as long as your 'inner you' is in agreement.
   b. **Review your placement again** and ask your 'inner you', 'Does this feel right?' Listen for the answer and adjust your picture accordingly.
   c. **Does your picture please you?** Look at your picture and see if it pleases you. If it does, the placements are probably right. If an area jars you, your reaction means that it probably needs some more work.

Well done! You have just created the first draft of your soul map.

Hints and Tips

- This is **not a process to be rushed.**
- As this is your soul map, expect yourself to be the family member with the **most lesson and relationship lines.**
- Look at your soul map again to see it as your **family sitting in a circle facing each other.** Who would sit next to each other and who would naturally start calling out to each other? Are they in easy line of sight of each other? If not, revise the placement. Is there an aunt always teasing an uncle, or two cousins who are

This is not
a process to
be rushed.

always sharing a private joke? This is possibly another grouping and could change where you choose to place them in your soul map. Are there any faces in your mind's picture of your family gathering that spring into view but are missing from your soul map? If your 'inner you' is in agreement, add them to your soul map.

- If the **picture pleases you,** you are doing the right things, so take confidence from that feeling. This process is about being honest with yourself. There is no one looking over your shoulder.
- Remember to **close down when you have finished** working on your Soul Family.

Expect to Revise Your Placement a Number of Times

Do remember that not all of your natural family will be in your soul map. Andrea had a brother-in-law and his daughter who were significant members of her family but not in her soul map. Andrea thought long and hard about whether this was correct. She concluded that her niece was very much like her father and his family. Therefore, she felt it correct that neither of them was part of her Soul Family.

What I have concluded is that soul families overlap much as they do in this life. Andrea's sister-in-law was part of her soul family, but her sister-in-law's husband and their daughter were part of her sister-in-law's Soul Family. I have drawn a diagram to help describe this type of situation.

There is another situation which may occur when you are looking at your life. I believe that our soul families are part of soul communities. If our life is a play, we need to find actors to take various roles in our life. Who else would you turn to but your immediate neighbours, who are known to you? Therefore, there can be peo-

Soul families overlap,
much as they do
in this life.

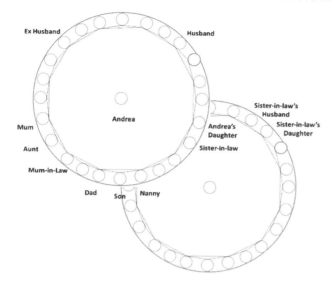

Figure 14. Andrea and her sister-in-law's overlapping soul families.

ple who come into your life, often at a pivotal time, and make an impact, sometimes changing the entire direction of your life, but who are not part of your direct Soul Family.

This is what had happened to Janie. Janie is a bank manager from Tokyo who has lived happily for many years in London. She was constructing her first soul map and considering who of her friends and family were in it. Janie had a dilemma: a former colleague from Tokyo was instrumental in helping her to decide to come to London, but she did not feel that he was part of her soul family. After she reflected on this relationship, she decided, *'I knew this person had made a real impact on my life, but I did not feel he was part of my Soul Family.'*

Once she had made the decision to move to the UK, this man drifted out of her life. Not keeping in touch with a person who

Soul families live in
soul communities.

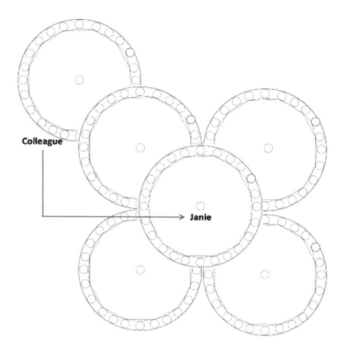

Figure 15. Soul communities.

has made such an impact on your life is not uncommon. His purpose had been achieved, so he did not feel the need to remain in Janie's life.

Chapter 5: You and Your Family Member Colours

In this phase you start to add colour to your soul map. Your map becomes much more vibrant and alive, reflecting who you and your family are.

The objective of this phase is:
- To take a first look at the colours of your Soul Family members.

Soul Colours

Members of your soul family talk to you showing themselves in a particular colour. I believe this relates to the colour of the chakra or energy centre from which they are speaking to you. I feel that there is value in understanding the basic meanings of the chakras to gain a better understanding of the nature of the communication from your family member.

There is value in understanding the basic meaning of the chakras to gain a better understanding of the nature of the communication.

Chakras

Originating in Hinduism and Tantric Buddhism, chakras are energy centres in our bodies through which energy flows. There are seven key ones which align with our spine up through our bodies. Each has a specific colour and shape and is associated with a specific organ and emotions. It is through our emotions that we speak with the universe and universal energy. Therefore, the emotion associated with a chakra can add meaning to the family member in your soul map with that colour. An example would be the members of Andrea's family she assigned with the colour yellow. Yellow is for confidence, self-worth, self-esteem and being in control of your life. The yellows in Andrea's soul map, in their individual ways, are all supporters of what she is trying to achieve in her life. At moments of self-doubt they are there to help her with her confidence. Let's take a look at each of the chakras:

Root Chakra – found at the base of our spine in the tail-bone area. Red in colour, it is our foundation and addresses survival issues such as food and money.

Sacral Chakra – found in the lower abdomen about two inches below the navel. Orange in colour, it is abundance, well-being, pleasure and sexuality.

Solar Plexus Chakra – found in the upper abdomen. Yellow in colour, it is our ability to be confident and in control of our lives. It gives us our self-worth, self-confidence and self-esteem.

Heart Chakra – found in the centre of the chest just above our heart. Green in colour, it is our ability to love. It gives us our love, joy and inner peace.

Throat Chakra – found in the throat. Blue in colour, it gives us our ability to communicate, express our feelings and the truth.

Third Eye Chakra – found in the forehead between the eyes. Indigo in colour, it is our intuition, imagination, wisdom, ability to think and make decisions.

Crown Chakra – found at the very top of the head. Mauve in colour, it is our connection to spirituality, pure bliss.

Figure 16. The chakras.

Chakra symbols.

Figure 16 shows a picture of the chakras. I have added the symbols to help anyone who may be colour blind.

In the following steps, we are going to determine the chakra colour of each of your family members. For this exercise, you will need some colour pens, chalks or Tiddlywinks counters that match the chakra colours. I think counters are the easiest to work with, as you can readily move them around until you have decided on which colours you associate with individual family members. To make things easier for you, I have added a page of coloured circles in the Resources appendix that you can copy and cut out to use as counters.

For those of you who may be colour blind, I suggest that you work with the chakra symbols. You can copy them from this book and cut them out like counters. You will find larger symbols in the Appendix for this purpose.

After Andrea did this exercise, her soul map looked like the one in Figure 17.

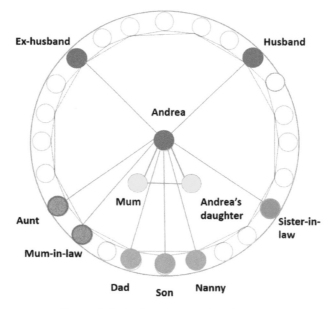

Figure 17. Andrea's soul map with soul colours.

Meditation to Assist with the Exercise

To help with this exercise in my workshops we do a guided meditation on either receiving energy from Mother Earth, feeling the energy flowing through our chakras, or colouring or aligning our chakras. These exercises seem to help us to connect with energy and the associated chakra colours. You might like to try this at home before you do this exercise. There are many good guided meditations available; just search on the internet for one that you like. Here are the basics for undertaking a meditation.

Meditating is simple yet challenging, as the techniques are easily learnt but the mind might not be so keen to follow them. The more you practise meditation, the easier it becomes. Meditation relies heavily on concentration:

- Before you start, find a quiet place where you will not be disturbed. Sit either on a chair or on a cushion on the floor.

- Place your feet firmly on the floor if sitting on a chair or cross your legs if you are on the floor. Straighten your back and rest your hands in your lap with palms uppermost.

- Breathe slowly and deeply from the diaphragm while relaxing and emptying the mind. Each time you breathe out, everything that is unpleasant and unwanted leaves you. Each time you breathe in, you are filled up with harmony, new vitality and peace.

- Visualise a root growing out of the base of your spine down into Mother Earth. Feel the energy from Mother Earth going up into you and refreshing you.

- Enjoy the energy as it moves up into your red root chakra. Pause and enjoy the energy you are being given. Feel the energy move up to the next chakra.

- Repeat this through the orange sacral chakra, yellow solar plexus chakra, green heart chakra, blue throat chakra, indigo third eye chakra and mauve crown chakra.

- If your attention wanders and distracting thoughts arise, let them drift away and bring your mind gently back to your chakras.

Meditation is simple but challenging.

The more you practise meditation, the easier it becomes.

- When you have reached your crown chakra, sit and enjoy the calmness. Continue like this initially for five minutes, building slowly up over time to twenty minutes.

- When you are ready, slowly bring your attention back to the world around you and to sitting in the chair or on the floor.

The art of meditation is to still the mind. Try to remain still for the duration of your meditation. Your mind may not like this, as it's used to being on the move and controlling your body. There will be perceived small discomforts which your mind will want you to move to relieve or there will be an urgent desire to scratch your nose or rub your face. These are all distracting techniques used by your mind to try to get you to move. Instead, try moving your attention from these distractions back to your chakras. The whole purpose of meditation is to free you of your restless mind and allow you to experience stillness.

If you are not into meditation, it's not a problem. Just move into the exercise.

To identify each of your individual family member's colours, follow these steps:

1. Lay out all the colours.
2. Select a few colours.
3. Identify family member colours.
4. Identify your own colour.
5. Review your family member colours.
6. Record your own and your family members' colours.

Detailed Steps for Identifying Your Family Member Colours

For the purpose of this exercise I will assume we are using chakra-coloured counters. Let's look at each step in more detail.

Mediation can free you of your restless mind and allow you to experience calmness.

1. **Lay out all the colours.**

Lay out one counter of each colour in front of you.

2. **Select a few colours.**

Look at the counters and see which you find most attractive. Some may seem to shine brighter, or you may just be attracted to some more than others. You should select one to three different colours, and a maximum of four at this stage.

If you are not sure which colours to choose, think of the colours in the home in which you grew up. Often these are the colours your family feel comfortable with. This was Andrea's experience:

'In my parents' home the dominant colour was blue, but my dad used to loved to bring yellow flowers into the home. At the time, I thought nothing of it other than it was rather nice that my dad still brought mum flowers. It's only in more recent times that I have come to realise that my dad's colour is blue and that my mum's is yellow. At a subconscious level, they were recognising and honouring each other's soul colour.'

How amazing is that – much more significant than 'nice'!

3. **Identify family member colours.**

Make a small pile of counters for each of your chosen colour(s).

   a. Pick up one of your selected counters and ask your 'inner you', 'Do any of my family members use this colour?' **Move the counter** over each family member in turn.

   b. **Wait to feel what seems right** and when you do, place the counter over that family member.

   c. **Repeat this process several times for the same colour** to see if there are any other members who use this colour.

Repeat this process for each colour counter. If you are not sure which colour is appropriate for a family member, just leave it blank

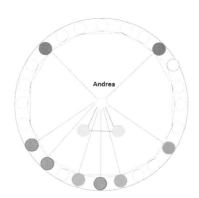

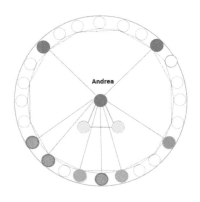

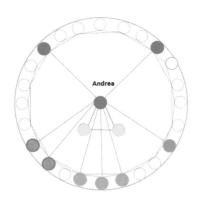

for now. This is not unusual at this stage. The right colour will come to you over time.

4. **Identify your own colour.**
   a. Lay out in front of you **one counter for each of the seven colours of the chakras.**
   b. Touch each one in turn and ask yourself '**Is this my colour?**' Wait for the answer. This is an important question. Close your eyes as you ask it. Sometimes doing so increases your ability to receive the reply.
   c. When you think you have identified your colour, **repeat the process** and see if you get the same result or a different answer.
   d. **If the answer is different,** leave yourself white and repeat this exercise another day.

5. **Review your family member colours.**
   • Sit back and review the results on your circle and feel if any adjustments are needed. Keep asking yourself, 'Does this feel right?'
   • Make adjustments as necessary.

6. **Record your colour and your family members' colours.**
   Colour yourself and your family members with felt pen or crayons on your soul map with the colours you have identified. You can now put your counters away. Keep them safe as you will find them useful in other exercises.

Hints and Tips
   • **Not every family member will have a colour** at this stage. This is all right and is to be expected.

- You will probably be working with **only one to three colours,** with a maximum of four. It's best to start this process with a small number.
- This **exercise can be repeated multiple times** over a number of weeks until you get a consistent answer.
- Do not be surprised if you want to **revise the location** of some of your family members as you do this exercise. It is quite common.
- Remember to **close down when you have finished** working on your Soul Family.

It was during this exercise that Andrea realised that her mum and her daughters were her key supporters and part of her inner circle. She revised her soul map to move them to the space one below her on the right and the other on the left. Creating a soul map is a journey, and insights will come to you as you progress. This development is good, as it means you are increasing your conscious awareness of yourself and strengthening communication with your 'inner you'. Please do not ignore the desire to make changes to your soul map in an effort to speed things along. It is important to follow your desires, as they reflect your true reality.

When you are happy with the result of this exercise, move onto the next phase.

ᔕᑎᘔ
Follow your desires,
as they reflect your
true reality.
ᔕᑎᘔ

Your Soul Family
aims to enhance
your conscious
awareness of
yourself

Enjoy the peace in your soul map

Chapter 5: How Are You Doing?

You have all the fundamentals of your soul map in place. Just look at what you have done so far. Congratulations! You have …

- **Identified key people** from your friends and families who you feel are part of your Soul Family. You may have some individuals you are not sure about· and you will need to consider them further as you progress.
- **Identified if there are any lessons** an individual may be learning and if anyone is helping them – for example, with improved communications.
- **Identified some special relationships** between Soul Family members – for example, the widows in Andrea's family.
- **Identified if you have an inner circle of supporters.**
- **Constructed your basic soul map** by placing family members in your soul map being guided by groupings of family members and lessons they are learning. You have learnt to talk to your 'inner you' to confirm where individuals should sit in your soul map.
- **Identified the colours** of some of your family members.
- **Identified your own colour.**

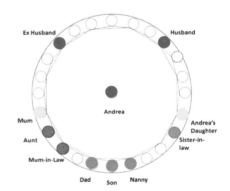

You have done so much. It never ceases to amaze me how much progress people can make with a few simple exercises. Students from my workshops say that they are amazed about how much they learn about themselves and their lives. The information is locked up within you — you just need to bring it into your conscious mind.

When I send a birthday card I always give it a kiss and send my love with it before I put it in the postbox. I often wondered if it was me being silly or whether my love was actually received by the recipient. It was only when I mentioned it to a friend of mine who is a medium that I found out the answer. It is her belief that when I kiss the envelope I am sending out a strong intention to send my love. My love is attached to the card and the recipient will receive it. If they are sensitive they will also be able to see the energy as a colour haze radiating from the card, but almost anyone can feel it. This is one of the reasons why we are so disappointed if someone forgets your birthday and does not send you a card. At the intuitive level, we miss receiving that feeling of being loved. My friend always keeps her cards of thanks, birthday good wishes, and others, and periodically she takes them out to have a look at them so she can enjoy again their energy of love.

The same will happen with your soul map. You are putting a lot of your energy and love into creating your soul map. Every time you take it out and look at it you will feel this love and the connection with your 'inner you'. Even at this stage of development, there is enough energy and love in your soul map to be worth reflecting on it and re-experiencing the insights and love in it. To gain more meaning, try looking again at the chakra colours and their associated emotions. Does this bring you any more insight about your family?

Kissing an envelope can send a strong intention of love.

Andrea believes in past lives. When she was exploring the colours in her soul map, this is what she discovered:

My dad, mother-in-law and son are all blue in colour and were grouped together on my soul map. This seemed an unlikely grouping in this life, so I asked the question of my 'inner you' what it was about. What I found out was that they needed in this life to have an honest conversation with each other about a past life relating to judgement. Sharing the colour blue coming into this life expressed their intention to have this conversation. Blue represents communication, expressing our feelings and the truth.

Whether you believe in past lives or not is immaterial. The colours, groupings and placements in your soul map will provide signals of the insight your 'inner you' is trying to give you. It never ceases to amuse me that you have to work so hard to gain your insights into who you are and where you are going. It is almost a test of the level of your desire to know yourself. I can see my mum smiling and reminding me of what she used to say to me as a child: 'Nothing worth having is not without work.' Thanks, Mum!

Over the coming weeks you can expect important thoughts and insights to come in. It greatly helps this process if you make time for quiet reflection so you are able to hear what your 'inner you' is saying to you above the noisy chatter of your brain. Often insight comes to you in the shower, as you go to sleep or as you wake up. Capture these insights right away, as they are easily forgotten and lost. It is really frustrating when you know you have received an insightful thought, but you cannot remember what it is! Figure 18 shows an example **Thought Diary** I suggest you might like to keep. The Resources appendix has a full-sized version.

'Nothing worth having is not without work.'

Date	Thought/Dream/Insight	Follow-up Action

Figure 18. Example Thought Diary.

The act of creating your soul map initiates a period of insights arriving. When I am in an active period, I keep a pen and piece of paper beside the bed and in the bathroom so I can jot down any key messages and then go back to sleep or continue my shower. Later in the day I then transfer the messages into my Thought Diary, giving some more attention to what they might mean. Thinking about them seems to keep the contact with my 'inner you' going, and sometimes I receive more information as I update my Thought Diary. It seems simple, but it is an effective technique.

Chapter 6: Family Dynamics Guide the Core Design of Your Soul Map

The circle at the centre of your soul map represents yourself and possibly some other family members around you if you have an inner circle of confidants and supporters. You may or may not have identified the colours for yourself and your inner circle. Now is the time to explore the remaining area in the core of your soul map. It is the heart of your soul map and therefore fundamental to understanding who you are.

The objective of this phase is:
- To finish designing the central part of your soul map.

In the central core of your soul map you are going to design a structure that matches the needs, desires and dynamics of your Soul Family. You have a choice of two approaches:

- Choosing a template from a range offered in this book and overlaying your soul map design.
- Develop your own design in consultation with your 'inner you'.

Both approaches are equally valid. You should choose the approach you are most comfortable with. Many people choose to use a template for their first soul map and after a period go on to create and colour a new soul map. Others feel too constrained by a template and want to jump right in and design their own. The choice is yours. Remember: This is your journey and one to be enjoyed, so choose the route that feels right for you and gives you the most pleasure.

In the next two chapters, we will go through each approach and provide some detailed steps on how to undertake the design. It might be useful to read these chapters before you make your choice on which approach to take.

Chapter 7: Choose a Template and Overlay Your Soul Map Design

There are two steps in this phase:

1. **Choose a template** that most closely matches your family's dynamics.
2. **Overlay your soul map design** on your chosen template and adjust the template where required.

Let's look at each step in more detail.

Choosing a Template That Most Closely Matches Your Family's Dynamics

In choosing your template to represent your family you can either be analytical or just feel what is right for you. How your family operates can guide you in your choice. In being analytical you can look at your family using the following pointers. Think about your family and decide:

- Does my family tend to have **multiple clusters, a few key people or many interactions?**
- Do I have an **inner circle of helpers?** Are they a select few or a larger group?

- Are there **many one-to-one relationships?**
- Does my family feel **in the midst of change,** or is it mature with significant wisdom?

Or you can use your intuition, your 'gut instinct', to ask your 'inner you' which feels the right template and choose it. Both methods work well, and a blend of both is even better. The key thing is not to agonise but to choose. Have confidence that you will make the right choice for you.

We have seven templates to choose from. Choose a template that you feel reflects the shape and dynamics of your family. If a template is not quite right for you, do not be afraid to change it. It is important that the template becomes your own. If none of the templates pleases you, remember that you can build the centre of your picture yourself. There is an eighth template, a foundation one, which you can use if you wish to take this route. If you decide to do so, skip to chapter 8.

Each template represents a shape from a different cultural and religious background. You can look at them and see which one seems most suitable as the basis of the first colouring of your soul map. Do not be surprised if you are attracted to a framework that does not reflect your own cultural or religious background. There will be a reason for your choice which will probably become apparent later on.

It is really important that you choose a framework that appeals to you and not one you feel you should choose simply because of your background or religion.

See which one resonates with you. Don't make a selection until you have gone through all of them. Be confident you have made the right choice for where you and your Soul Family are at this moment in time.

Choose a template that reflects the shape and dynamics of your family.

Have confidence you will make the right choice for you.

Daffodil-Inspired Template

Sometimes nature can help us to decide what would be an appropriate shape for the inner portion of our soul map. The daffodil blooms in the spring and represents new beginnings. This soul map contains the geometric shapes found in a daffodil.

Figure 19. A daffodil.

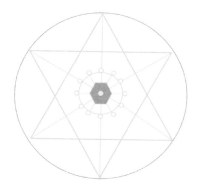

Figure 20. The structure of the daffodil forms the foundation of the Daffodil Template.

Figure 21. Daffodil-inspired template.

This family has six key family members and a strong inner circle to support you. The two equilateral triangles that join the six key family members represent achieving or practising balance within the family.

Celtic Cross–Inspired Template

This framework has two powerful symbols, the circle and the cross. The outer circle of life is re-emphasised by the inner circles and symbolises the endless path of knowledge. The cross represents the physical world and resides within these circles. The arms of the cross signify the north, south, east and west.

Figure 22. Celtic cross.

Figure 23. Replica Celtic broach.

This family feels strong and is very grounded and practical. You have a small number of supporters in your inner circle, but they are significant in your life. You know and understand each other well.

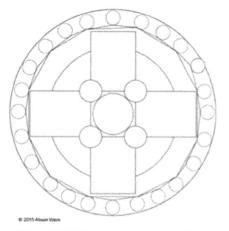

Figure 24. Celtic cross–inspired template.

Tibetan Buddhism-Inspired Template

Mandalas are an ancient Eastern art form, originating around the 9th century. Traditional mandalas, often created by Buddhist monks, can be deeply elaborate representations of nirvana. The word 'mandala' is a Sanskrit word meaning 'circle' or 'enclosure'. It was first recorded in the ancient Hindu scripture Rig Veda. However, it is with the Buddhist tradition, in particular Tibetan Buddhism, that mandalas are most commonly associated.

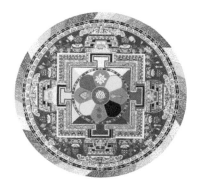

Figure 25. Example of a Tibetan mandala by an anonymous Tibetan painter.

The template in Figure 26 is inspired by the Tibetan mandala, which contains a square within the circle to represent the knowledge that the teacher wants to give to the pupil. In this framework the multiple lines represent the Life Lessons and skills available within the family, which provides opportunities for wisdom to be available to you. You are represented by the figure in the centre and supported by two key family members. The multiple connections you have to your outer circle are a mix of passed family members, your generation and the next. This arrangement serves to remind you of the transient nature of life.

This family has learnt many Life Lessons and has wisdom available to them. However, they do not always remember their lessons and use the skills available to them. They are reaching out to each other to improve their overall learning and recall their Life Lessons. You are a central figure in this process, and the figure in the centre of this soul map represents you.

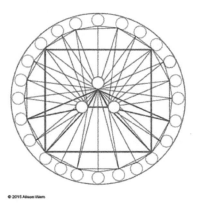

© 2015 Alison Wern

Figure 26. Tibetan Buddhism–inspired template.

Hexagram-Inspired Template

The hexagram is a pair of overlaid equilateral triangles and creates a six-pointed star with a hexagon in the middle. It is known as the Star of David in Judaism and is a Hindu mandala symbol called 'Sadkona Yantra'. It is a widely used symbol and is found in Christianity, including the Latter-Day Saints (Mormons), and in Islam, Theosophy, and the occult.

Figure 27. Example of a Sadkona Yantra.

The upward-pointing triangle is masculine and represents fire, while the downward triangle is feminine and represents water. The top half of the upward triangle interlocking with the base of the downward triangle is the symbol for air. The base of the upward triangle interlocking with the apex of the downward triangle is the symbol for Earth. This framework has the four elements of fire, water, air and earth. The interplay of upward and downward pointing triangles creates balance. The circle is both eternity and the route through which you travel to find your 'inner you'.

The two interlocking triangles are also the centre of the Heart Chakra symbol, which has twelve lotus petals around it. You'll recall that in Hinduism and Tantric Buddhism, a chakra is an energy centre in our bodies through which energy flows. The Heart Chakra is either green or pink and is associated with emotions, love and compassion. The downward pointing triangle and circle at the centre of this template is part of the Throat Chakra symbol and represents the ability to communicate.

© 2015 Alison Wern

Figure 28. Hexagram-inspired template.

This family is trying to or has achieved some balance and is practising unconditional love. Achieving inner peace is a core value of this family. The small triangles within the hexagram represent accumulated human experiences this family has attained. Their presence in this soul map serves to remind the family of the experiences through which they have learnt or are learning their Life Lessons, acquiring greater insight and wisdom. They are integral to achieving inner peace and harmony.

Interlocking Circles: An Islam-Inspired Template

The shape of a mosque is often based on five domes arranged around a double axis. They can be adorned with more domes, depending on the size and grandeur of the mosque. However, the core shape often remains the same. A circle in 3D is a dome which reflects the transition between Earth and the heavens.

Figure 29. Sultan Ahmed (Blue) Mosque, Istanbul.

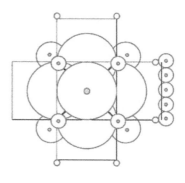

Figure 30. Sultan Ahmed (Blue) Mosque floor plan.

This family has many members clustered at the heart of the family. You are supported by four key family members, who in turn are supported by a further three. Supportive emotionally of one another, this family offers practical support when facing out into the physical world. This practical strength comes from the underlying equilateral cross, which is the foundation of this template.

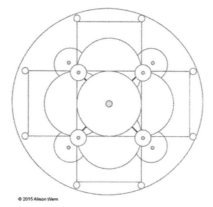

© 2015 Alison Wem

Figure 31. Interlocking circles in the Islam-inspired template.

Balance, Symmetry and Infinity-Inspired Template

Like the Sri Yantra diagram in the Hindu faith, this framework, shown in Figure 33, draws the eye to the centre as if through a tunnel, reflecting humanity's journey through the cosmos and taking us back to the moment of creation. The centre represents the beginning: the universe, our family, ourselves. The triangles represent physical existences which make up our world. For each family member in the rim there are multiple triangles. They have had many life experiences and opportunities to learn. The circle symbolizes that this has been happening for a long time. Our world expressed in geometric shapes and mathematical formulae helps us to understand it and to appreciate the balance and symmetry within it. The universe and the cosmos stretch out into infinity, as represented at the central point of the template.

Figure 32. Example of a Sri Yanta.

This family has acquired much wisdom from life experiences. The family members are joined in a circle and work with all in their family rather than in key hubs. They are comfortable sharing within their family group. This template shows that you have an inner circle of supporters who have been with you for as long as you can remember.

© 2015 Alison Wern

Figure 33. Balance, symmetry and infinity–inspired template.

Spiral-Inspired Template

Spirals are found all around us in nature and have had a significant place in the human psyche since the Stone Age.

Figure 34. Nature's spirals.

Ancient peoples were fascinated by spirals. A good example can be seen at the megalith passage tomb called the Mound of Hostages (Duma na nGial) on the Hill of Tara, County Meath, Ireland. It is the oldest monument on the Hill of Tara, dating back to between 2500 and 3000 BC. There is a wonderful spiral-decorated stone at the entrance gate. Their meaning is not known, but it is thought that perhaps the engravings represent the Sun, Moon or stars as religious symbols, or perhaps the stone was used as a prehistoric calendar.

The interlocking triple spiral represents the meeting of sky, earth and water, the intertwining of the past, present and future, and the progress of learning and acquiring knowledge. Balance and movement co-exist, coming together in the calmness of the centre.

Figure 35. Hill of Tara, reflecting the ancient Interest in spirals.

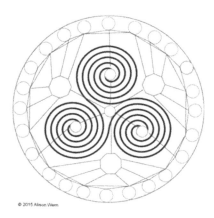

© 2015 Alison Wern

Figure 36. Spiral-inspired template.

This family is in the process of change. The triple spiral represents transformation. The family is learning from life events experienced by family members and are adapting their behaviour and learning new skills. You have three key supporters in your inner circle, and each in turn is the lead person in key clusters within the family. You have a second circle of supporters at the centre to help the family maintain its balance as they transform. You are central to holding the whole together and the point from which the calmness radiates outwards.

Overlay Your Soul Map Design on Your Chosen Template and Adjust the Template Where Required

This process creates an upgraded version of your soul map and is the design you will take forward into colouring. You will be moving your family members to the template, adjusting the template or the placement of your family members to create your best representation of your Soul Family. Your 'inner you' will guide you throughout this development. You will need to use your colour counters again for this exercise.

There are three steps for moving to your enhanced soul map:

1. Place yourself in the middle of your chosen template.
2. Place your family members into your template.
3. Step back from the soul map and feel if people are in the right place.

Here are the steps in more detail.

1. **Place yourself in the middle of your chosen framework.** It is your picture, after all! Take a colour counter for your colour and place it over the circle at the centre of the soul map. Within your soul map is a sacred space for you where you can find peace and tranquillity.

2. **Place your family members into your chosen template.** Using your basic soul design, take the relevant colour counter for each family member in turn and move them to your chosen template. Move your inner circle first, asking your 'inner you' for each person what is the most appropriate position for them on the inner circle of the template. Do not worry if you do not have a full set of family members for the template you have chosen. More insight will come over time on who they are or if they

Within your soul map is a sacred space for you where you can find peace and tranquillity.

even belong in your soul map. Likewise, if there are not enough circles for all the people in your inner circle, adjust the template to make space for them. Move each of your family members in turn while consulting your 'inner you'. Once again, do not worry if you do not use all of the available circles in the rim.

3. **Step back from the soul map and feel if people are in their right place.** Look at your soul map as a picture and see what it looks like. Does it feel right? Do you need to make any adjustments? If so, make them. Move people around your circle until you feel they are in the right positions.

Consider Symmetry, Balance and Structure

Does your picture look pleasing to you? Is it balanced? Is it symmetrical? If the picture is not symmetrical or balanced, ask yourself if that is important to you. Decide if you want a picture that is balanced, or one that perhaps more accurately represents the feelings in your family. Perhaps the family aspires to being more balanced.

Does your picture look pleasing to you?

Look at the relationships of your inner circle with the outer circle of people

Doing this can provide new insight about individuals, their relationships and/or their Life Lessons. Adjust positioning and label relationship/life lesson lines to reflect your new insight.

The power of three

Observation has shown that family members can make use of the power of three when placing themselves in your soul map. Placing individuals in groups of three can assist the building of your picture. Consult with your 'inner you' to check if this feels right.

Keep reviewing your picture and making adjustments until you feel happy with the way it looks and feels to you.

You have now transformed the template into the design of your soul map for colouring. If you used colour counters for placing your family members, record their names in the correct position and colour the circle with a crayon or felt pen before you remove the counters. Make sure you label any lines with the relationships or Life Lessons your 'inner you' has informed you of. This detailed design can contain quite a lot of information. You can either put all of the detail on the diagram or update your Family Information Table, whichever you prefer. The most important thing is that you do not lose the richness of this information. I find that students can forget the detail over time, and it is useful to be able to refer back to it. It is worth keeping a folder to put the papers from your Soul Family work in for safe-keeping. I usually date each exercise so I can see how my understanding has evolved over time. It gives me a mental pat on the back when I review my development over the multiple versions, something I find encouraging.

Hints and Tips

- You can be **analytical in your choosing** of a template or rely on your intuition – both approaches work well. A blend of both can work better.
- Choose a **template that feels right** for you rather than one that you think matches your current cultural background.
- In choosing a template **do not agonise**. Be confident you will have chosen the right one for you.
- Remember to **close down when you have finished** working on your Soul Family.

Chapter 8: Design the Central Part of Your Soul Map

If you choose to design your own central area to your soul map, you can use our Foundation Template to help you start and follow the exercises in this chapter to help develop your design. If you have decided to use a significant variation on one of the templates provided, the steps in this chapter may be helpful to you as well. The Foundation Template is available in the Resources appendix or can be downloaded from www.yoursoulfamily.com.

As you design your soul map it is worth remembering that your 'inner you' appreciates balance and symmetry. Your design is likely to please you more if it is organised and balanced rather than chaotic.

The objective of this phase is:
* To create your own design for the inner core of your soul map in consultation with your 'inner you'.

It is important that the design of your picture rises from your 'inner you' as if given to you by some power greater than the conscious you. Be patient – it may take several attempts before a design speaks directly to you.

Your design should rise from your 'Inner You' as if given to you by some power greater than the conscious you.

Take your soul map as it currently stands and place the Foundation Template next to it. Ask your 'inner you' what the structure of the inner core should look like. For some people, the ideas then start to flow and you should use a pencil and sketch them on the Foundation Template. Other people find that they need some inspiration to help them.

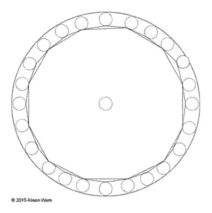

© 2015 Alison Wem

Figure 37. Foundation Template.

Intuition-Led Design

At one of my workshops, Gerry, a successful business man from Sevenoaks with two small children, decided to customise his template design:

'I immediately felt the templates were too constraining for me. Using my intuition to do my own design I knew was the right route for me.'

Gerry sketched his ideas freehand on a Foundation Template and played with coloured counters to ensure that the placement and colours of his family members felt correct. Then he reproduced a neater design using a ruler for the lines and coins to create the circles for his inner circle of family members. This is the version he painted. The result was very pleasing to him and his 'inner you' and closely represented his family's dynamics.

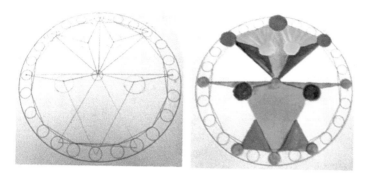

Figure 38. Gerry's design and coloured soul map.

Many people use the power of Microsoft software to help with building their neat version of their own soul map design. A soft copy of the Foundation Template can be downloaded from the website www.yoursoulfamily.com.

Structures in Nature Can Inspire Your Design

Depending on where you live, go out into the country or to the florist or a supermarket and look at some flowers. Take your camera or smartphone with you. Look at the centre of the flowers and notice the variety of geometric structures they have. If a particular flower speaks to you, take a picture of it or, better still, buy it if you can. Then go home and use its structure to guide the shape and structure of your soul map.

I live in London, so I went along to my allotment in search of flowers to take pictures for my students. Here is a collage of my favourite selection of flowers (see Figure 39). Notice the variety of geometric shapes – pentagons, hexagons, spirals in endless variety. The trick is not to hesitate in selecting the flower for you but to choose and be confident you have made the right choice. If the flower appeals to you, your 'inner you' is agreeing with you.

Figure 39. Collage of flowers with different geometric structures.

I kept prompting
Andrea to keep looking
more deeply at
her chosen flower.

When I did this exercise with Andrea, she chose a daffodil. I kept prompting her to keep looking more deeply at her chosen flower. Here are my notes on how Andrea progressed. This later became our Daffodil template.

Daffodil Exercise

Andrea had already built and painted one soul map, but she felt compelled to draw another one. I have found that this is not unusual when change or transformation is happening to you. This is how Andrea described her experience:

The spring was coming and we had a vase of daffodils in our sitting room. Daffodils are a poignant flower for me and represent old chapters finishing in my life and new ones starting. At the time of my father's passing he spent the last week in bed. He was a man who loved to be outside, so we put a large vase of beautiful yellow daffodils in his room so he could feel the coming of the spring.

Figure 40. Daffodil photo.

Some years later, when I was feeling very alone, I received a message to say something wonderful would happen to me at the time of the daffodils. Sure enough, I met my husband and found new love just as the daffodils started to bloom.

As the daffodil is so significant to me, I decided to try the geometric shape exercise using it. It did not take me a long time to get the initial framework. I felt very pleased and excited with the result as it reflected important facets of my life – new beginnings and the relationships I had with key loved ones.

Looking at the flower, Andrea noted the geometric shapes within it, plus the symmetry and balance. She wanted to replicate that pattern in her picture. Starting with the outer circle, which she felt reflected the eternal nature of our lives, Andrea then added the geometry of the daffodil.

The tips of the petals had a deeper yellow colour. Andrea felt that the petal points connected her to key loved ones in her family who had an important part to play in her development and life, so she added them to her picture.

Andrea felt she was loved by many people, so she added them to her outer circle. There are many inter-relationships between the members of her loved ones, so she added an inner circle which is made up of many lines connecting her loved ones and representing these relationships.

Andrea looked at the daffodil again to see if it could give her any more information about herself. Focus on the picture of the daffodil to really get the feel for its structure and geometry. What she saw was that the rim around the trumpet of the daffodil had an uneven edge. Andrea interpreted this as her having an inner circle of particular friends within her circle of loved ones. This was a new idea to Andrea. With the stamen being herself at the centre of her inner circle, she added her friends to her picture and some lines to represent the relationships between them. Andrea thought about who might be in her inner circle. From earlier work she knew her mother and daughter were part of this group, but who else should be there? She immediately thought of a dear friend who has worked with her on overcoming her life challenges 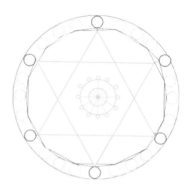 and who has encouraged her to express her thoughts and ideas. She named her friend as part of her special inner circle. The others remained unnamed, but she decided to work on that aspect later.

Andrea had a final look at her daffodil to gather more information. She noted some lines in the petals, which she felt were significant, but she was unsure how they connected individuals in terms of relationships and lessons as only the central line touched two souls. Andrea decided to add only these con-  necting lines to her picture. She would consider the remaining lines and add them to her picture when their meaning became apparent to her, as she felt sure they would at a later time. Never feel pushed into adding something to your picture if at that time it does not feel right to you. When you desire to add a feature, that is when the time is right for you.

On her daffodil, Andrea also noted a darker area around the stamen. At first, she thought it was another circle but when she looked closely she realised it was a hexagon. She did not realise at this point that the hexagon was important for the birth of her next soul map. Andrea was amazed and excited to realise  how fundamental geometric shapes are to our world. In response Andrea changed her inner circle to add this shape to her picture, providing it with the correct spacing for her inner circle of loved ones. This addition created more structural symmetry and balance. It made her picture feel structurally sound and strong, in the same way that her inner circle of souls provides support and strength to her life.

Andrea sat back and looked at the geometric design for her personalised soul map: *'I was amazed at the amount of detail and pleased by the shape, balance and symmetry of my soul map. It felt like a good design for me to now colour.'*

It is interesting to note that the healing properties of the daffodil flower remedy are to assist in meditation and to stimulate connection to your soul.[2] It increases clarity of thought, promotes optimism and eases social interactions.

---

2 **Flower remedies:** 38 flower remedies were defined by Dr Edward Bach in the 1930s to alleviate mental conditions. Daffodil essence was not one of those remedies but has become popular in recent years. The Practical Herbalist and One Willow internet apothecaries have the history of the daffodil remedy and more details on its benefits.

Typical Geometric Shapes Used in Soul Map Designs

Here are some suggestions of shapes you can use in your soul map design. You can buy an inexpensive template in your local stationers that has these shapes. Alternatively, you can use the time-proven tools of a compass and ruler. **Let your flower guide the overall shape of your design.** Here are some examples of doing this.

Figure 41. Spiral example.   Figure 42. Star example.   Figure 43. Five-point star example.

Now consider whether you would like to use some **geometric shapes to enhance your soul map design.** Typical shapes include triangles, squares, circles, and hexagons. As always, do what pleases you and consult with your 'inner you'.

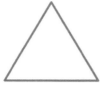

Figure 44. Basic soul map geometric shapes.

Sarah, a teacher from an inner London school, successfully designed her own soul map design. This was her second soul map: *'I found it hard to get going, but once I started the design seemed to flow. I am really pleased with the result. My life has changed so much in the last six months, so this soul map is very different from my original one and reflects where I am in life.'*

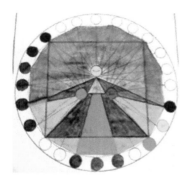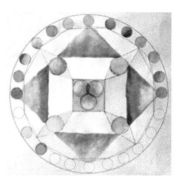

Figure 45. Sarah's first soul map.   Figure 46. Sarah's second soul map.

Overlay the Information from Your Earlier Design onto Your Tailored Design

It is highly likely that you were thinking about your family members and the dynamics of their relationships as you created your design. At the time of design, you may be very clear on the colour associated with each family member and where they are located in your soul map. However, memory is not always accurate over time, and it would be a shame to lose the richness of your work. Therefore, at the end of your design activity, record the individual members' names, relationships or lessons onto your design, along with their colour. Alternately, record the detail in your Family Information Table. I always like to put the date on the design, making it is easy to see your progress if you feel the need to make more changes as new insights come to you. As with the template design, it is good to keep all of this information in a folder.

Throughout this process do not forget to put your dreams, thoughts and insights into your Thought Diary.

Hints and Tips

- If the **templates feel too constraining** for you or you have already done a template design, this is the right approach for you.
- **Let yourself enjoy building your soul map design.** If it feels too difficult, put it away and take it out another day.
- **Let your creativity loose.** This is the time to truly follow whatever feels right.
- Expect to **revisit your design** and make changes.
- Carefully **record the detail of your design** so you can review it later.
- **Date your designs** so you can see your progress.
- Remember that **your 'inner you' is always with you** and ready to help you if asked.
- Remember to **close down when you have finished** working on your Soul Family.

Have fun building your soul map. Take your time, play with it, meditate and think about the visual picture of your soul map and make changes. Above all, make the process your own. Do not be afraid to

Remember that your 'inner you' is always with you and ready to help if asked.

Remember to close down when you have finished working.

change the approach, the picture, colours or other features. I have described how the process has worked for my students, but we are all individual; use whatever is right for your design.

For my earliest students, building their soul maps took some time since they were trail-blazing. However, I am anticipating that with the support provided in this book, your soul map will take form at whatever pace suits you. Put in the time on this work that suits you and your life. Do not rush it and add pressure that is not necessary. Take your time to learn to listen to guidance from your 'inner you'. Andrea had a few false starts and decided to adjust her design further, but she got there in the end. Andrea always felt very positive about her efforts and about each step she took. Her 'inner you' was always very supportive and never critical. Looking back, she could see that some of her early attempts were quite basic, but she always felt a sense of approval, never disappointment. What mattered was that she was trying. You should remember this as you set out to build your own soul map: the most important thing about your work is that you are trying. Andrea did not work on her picture all the time but kept revisiting it and making changes that pleased her.

Above all, enjoy building your soul map design.

ℰↃℂℛ
Use whatever is
right for you to
inspire your design.
ℰↃℂℛ

Chapter 9: Colour Your Soul Map

I am always so excited when someone starts to colour their soul map. Adding colour brings your map to life, and adding your choice of colour and energy makes it very personal to you. This stage is the culmination of all the preparation you have done so far, so make sure you savour it.

Objectives of this phase are:
- To represent each family member's energy as accurately as possible in your soul map.
- Relaxation, calmness and fun.

In my experience, this is a very relaxing stage in the process. In this relaxed state, more information will come to you. You will gain greater knowledge of the lessons you are learning. Observing my students, I have noticed they always found this fresh knowledge came to them as it became relevant to them in their lives, especially when they were asking questions such as:

'Why did that challenge arrive? What am I trying to learn?' or

'Why did that person behave towards me like they did? Is there learning for me in this interaction?'

This is a very relaxing stage in the process.

When you ask a simple and explicit question, an answer will come. If you listen, the same will happen to you.

Let's re-cap. You have created the design for your soul map, added the information you know about your family and perhaps started to understand the colour of individuals in your Soul Family. You are now ready to add colour to the body of the picture.

Detailed Steps to Colouring Your Soul Map

Adding colour to your soul map is not a process to rush. Contemplate your soul map, choose a colour and decide where it needs to be applied. You do not need great artistic skills, as you are essentially colouring in geometric shapes. My students repeatedly confirm that this process brings great calmness. Whenever they speak of painting their picture there is always a smile on their faces and a look of serenity.

Try to choose a time and place to colour your picture when you will not be interrupted and can enjoy doing this activity. It is something special just for you, a real gift from your 'inner you' to you. Figure 47 shows some examples from my students.

1. **Choose a medium to colour with and experiment with it.**
2. **Colour your family members and yourself.**
3. **Choose background colours and add them to your soul map.**
4. **Fix the colours on your soul map.**

Let's look at each step in more detail:

1. **Choose a medium to colour with and experiment with it.** It could be watercolour paint, acrylic paint, chalk, crayons or felt pens. Choose what feels right for you. I like watercolours or acrylic paint because they are easy to obtain and use, and because I feel they add more vibrancy than a child's crayon. Paint is easy

Students repeatedly confirm that this process brings great calmness.

No artistic skills are required. You are colouring geometric shapes.

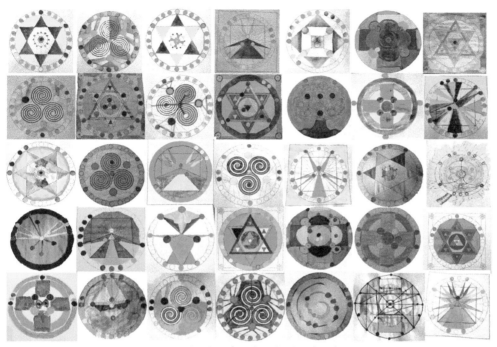

Figure 47. Selection of students' painted soul maps.

to blend to create different shades to help you more accurately capture how family members present their energy to you. And paint makes it easier to represent family members who might have a greater density of colour at their core than at their rim.

Using paints to good effect seems to engage the brain more than other colouring mediums. I have noticed that students using paints find it easier to hear their 'inner you', as I believe the mind is busy with the painting – work which keeps its noisy chatter quiet!

Experiment with the medium you want to use to add colour. The aim of this is to understand the effect the medium has and how

Experiment with the medium you want to use to add colour.

you might blend and mix colours. If your chosen medium does not produce the result you are looking for, do not be afraid to try a different one.

2. **Colour your family members and yourself.** Traditionally, you paint the background and then the foreground. I do not know why, but a lot of students like to colour their family members first and then themselves. I can only assume that the family members add structure and colour to their soul map, making it easier to decide on the appropriate energy colour to surround them. Let's review the activities in this step in the popular order.

Before you start to colour, address your 'inner you' and ask this question:

'What is the message that I should hear at this moment in my life?'

Once you have asked it, focus on colouring. Asking this question invites your 'inner you' to provide you with guidance, which will arrive in the coming days.

The representation of a family member may not be a single colour, just as with your counters. Consider if individual family members have slightly different shades – darker or lighter, or, for example, a deep cerise pink that has a touch of blue in it or a blue tending towards lilac. Do some family members have a darker centre with a lighter rim?

You might like to take all of the family members with the same core colour as a group and consider the different shades they might have. Then colour them, remembering to sit back periodically and review the effect on your soul map and asking your 'inner you' if the effect is pleasing. Do not be afraid to change your map if it does not please you, even if you have to wait for paint to dry before you paint over it.

Try to disengage your brain and let your eyes work with the different visual effects your brush can produce. You may want to experiment on a copy of your design before you paint your soul map.

If you have a family member whose colour you are not sure about, paint the outline of their circle in blue but let the inner part be part of the background colour of your soul map. If you understand their colour later you can add it then.

If you are using a template and you have family member circles for people you have not identified, just leave them uncoloured at this stage.

3. **Choose the background colours and add them to your soul map.** You've now coloured your soul map to reflect all of the members as well as yourself. Next you need to decide on the background colours for your picture. This is the time to lose yourself in your picture and just paint whatever colours feel good. These colours represent the energy moving around your family. For family member circles with no-one identified, just paint over them. You can add them back in as you identify them at a later date.

When you have finished adding colour to your soul map, sit back and contemplate it. Feel the extra energy that colour has brought to your family. What thoughts come to you? Make sure you capture them in your diary. Additional thoughts may come to you in the next couple of days as you think about your picture. Be sure you capture them, as they will be important to you.

ഇൻ
Take all the family members with the same core colour as a group.
ഇൻ

ഇൻ
Feel the extra energy that colour has brought to your family.
ഇൻ

Over time your ideas about your soul map colours may change and you may want to paint the same design again. This is good – it means your knowledge is evolving. It's all part of your journey and development.

4. **Fix the colours on your soul map.** If you have chosen water colours as your colouring medium, once your painting is dry spray your soul map well with cheap hair spray. This will help to fix the colours and prevent them from fading. After all your hard work you do not want your soul map to lose its energy!

As with each stage in this process, a new step can bring fresh insight. Remember to note any key thoughts or insights in your Thought Diary. If it changes your design you will need to adjust your soul map and capture the information in your Family Information Table or the detailed design. Do remember to date the change and file the design in your folder.

Guidance from the question you asked your 'inner you' will arrive in the coming days. It may come in some unexpected ways – as a knowing, a dream, a phrase on the radio echoing a thought or a billboard picture or words jumping out at you. Be alert so you are able to receive your message when it chooses to arrive.

If after a while you are unsure whether you have received your message correctly, repeat the question again while you are reflecting on your soul map. Wait to see what answer you get. If the message is the same as the original one, it is highly likely you received it correctly. This is not a process to rush. Take your time to receive your message.

Guidance from the question you asked your 'Inner You' will arrive in the coming days.

Hints and Tips

- **Experiment** and see what different effects you are able to achieve with your chosen colouring material.
- Many of us have not used paints in a long time – often since childhood. Do not use too much water, **just wet your brush rather than soak it.** You only need a **small amount of paint to colour** your family member. **Experiment with mixing a colour.**
- If the colouring material does not give you the effect you want, **do not be afraid to change to another one.**
- Think about the **nature of your family** – is it lively, contemplative or passionate? Decide which colours or mix of colours best represents this energy.
- Remember to **close down when you have finished** working on your Soul Family.
- **A family is dynamic and the colours or energy** will change as it responds to events, lessons, emotions. This picture is for today, so paint your family as it is today.
- **Relax and enjoy yourself.** This is time for you.

ೞ೦೮೩
A family is dynamic, and
the colours or energy
will change as it responds
to events, lessons
and emotions.
ೞ೦೮೩

Feel the energy colour
brings to your soul map

Allow your calmness to arrive

Chapter 10: Reflecting on Your Soul Map

After you have created your soul map, using it to reflect on or in meditation will continue to strengthen the communication with your 'inner you'. Reflecting on your soul map you find again that quiet space within you where you can meet and communicate with your 'inner you'. You will be able to ask a question and receive an answer. The more you practise it, the easier the dialogue becomes. To achieve my best thoughts, I now find it better to follow this process to step out of the bustle of everyday life, even if only for a few moments. At work there can be a tendency to be less connected while you are grappling with the challenges of business or caring for a family. However, just taking a few moments to reconnect with your 'inner you' before a key meeting, task, presentation, or speech can significantly enhance how you handle it and therefore help you to achieve the outcome you desire.

Here is one way to conduct this reflection. Some students record these words and play them back so they do not have to think about what they need to do. Do whatever is the easiest way for you.

Before you start, find a quiet place where you will not be disturbed. Sit, preferably at a table so you can prop up your picture where you can easily see it or on a cushion on the floor with your

Reflecting on your soul map you find again that quiet space within you.

picture in front of you. Place your feet firmly on the floor if you're sitting on a chair or cross your legs if you are on the floor. Straighten your back and rest your hands in your lap with palms uppermost. Now we are ready to begin.

- **Breathe slowly and deeply** from the diaphragm while relaxing and emptying the mind.
- Gently gaze at your soul map and relax your eyes so the picture goes into soft focus. Blink only as often as is necessary.
- **Thank your 'inner you'** for helping you to create it.
- Sitting quietly, **concentrate on your soul map,** taking in the shapes, patterns and colours and allowing them to work on your unconscious mind. If distracting thoughts arise, let them drift away and bring your mind gently back to your soul map.
- Initially take in the whole picture but then **let your eyes rest on one point.** The eyes are often drawn to the calmness at the centre of the picture. This is quite normal.
- **Continue to focus on that point for a few minutes.**
- **Move your eyes across your whole soul map.** Take in each family member and remember how they relate to you. You may wish to linger with a particular person and have a conversation. Be thankful they are in your life helping you with your Life Lessons.
- **Remember the insight** you received as you created your soul map and the feelings you experienced when you coloured it. Remember the relaxation and calmness, and savour it again.
- **In that calm space, you will be able to ask key questions about your life** to receive fresh insight.
- Continue like this initially for **five minutes, building up slowly over time to twenty minutes.**
- When you are ready, **slowly bring your attention back to the world around you** and to sitting in the chair or on the floor.

Bob, a retired businessman from New York in the US, describes his experience of his first reflection with his soul map: *'As my eyes went across my soul map and came to rest in the centre, the calmness returned. All the insight gained on my life came flooding back to me. It was amazing.'*

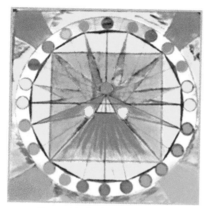

Figure 48. Andrea's soul map.

This is the soul map Andrea came to love and cherish. She took it with her whenever she travelled. She kept it in a plastic wallet to ensure it did not get damaged.

Soul Maps Are Also Useful in Moments of Stress

I used to keep my soul map on my desk at work when I was in a stressful corporate job. Whenever everything was chaotic I used to cast my eyes across my soul map and feel my calmness return, as though my 'inner you' had given me a big hug. I was then able to cope with my chaotic world more readily.

The kitchen is also a popular location for a soul map. Families often congregate in the kitchen and important conversations in your life often happen there. Your kitchen soul map can bring you

Whenever everything was chaotic, I used to cast my eyes across my soul map and feel my calmness return.

ෂ○Ცჳ

Cast your eyes across
your soul map and feel
your calmness return.

ෂ○Ცჳ

calmness in handling your life at home. It is quite all right to paint several soul maps so you can have one in several locations. It is not unusual to find that you have emphasised different colours in your soul maps if your needs are different in each location.

Staying connected to your 'inner you' greatly improves the quality of your thoughts. As a working wife, my mum used to dedicate one day a week to cleaning the house from top to bottom and getting the laundry washed, dried and ironed. As a child, I can remember thinking what a shame that my mum spent her mid-week day at home dedicated to monotonous housework. However, the reality was very different. My mum felt that the monotony of the work allowed her mind to relax and wander wherever it wanted to go. It was a luxury to have time to just 'be'. She said that it was on her Wednesdays at home that she had her best thoughts on what she wanted to do with her life, how she could help her family and generally make all of our lives more enjoyable. I am convinced she was having a day-long therapy chat with her 'inner you'.

ෂ○Ცჳ

Staying connected with
your 'Inner You' greatly
improves the quality of
your thoughts.

ෂ○Ცჳ

Different people do different things to stay in touch with their 'inner you'. A friend who lives alone is very close to nature. She always plans a walk through the fields near her house every day to ensure her personal well-being. If she is having a down moment she gives a tree a hug. She is slightly shy about this in case anyone should see her and think she is strange. However, on a cold winter's day she says the tree is surprisingly warm and provides her with comfort. The closeness of the tree is reassuring and refreshes her for the challenges of the coming day.

Everyone needs to find their own way of staying in touch with their 'inner you' and not feel embarrassed about it or worried about the time it takes. The benefits are so worthwhile.

Chapter 11: Personal Development and Growth

The human race and nature are much more closely connected than many of us recognise. In nature there is an ideal rate and pattern for achieving optimal growth. It is seen in flowers, leaf arrangements in plants and fruits such as pineapples. They all display instances of the mathematical Fibonacci sequence. You have to ask yourself whether optimal human personal growth also makes use of Fibonacci numbers and might be reflected in the shape of your soul map.

The Fibonacci sequence is a set of numbers that starts with a 1 or a 0, followed by a 1, and proceeds based on the rule that each number (called a Fibonacci number) is equal to the sum of the preceding two numbers, thus: 0, 1, 1, 2, 3, 5, 8 …

On average the number of petals in a flower matches one of the Fibonacci numbers. The correspondence is very exact with sunflowers, pine cones and pineapples. In many cases, the head of a flower is made up of small seeds which are produced at the centre and migrate outwards to eventually fill all of the space. Each new seed appears at a certain angle in relation to the preceding one. To maximise the efficiency of filling the space the angle needs to match the golden mean. These are the fractions that make up the

Figure 49. Sunflower head with a double spiral.

angles that approximate to the golden mean: 2/3, 3/5, 5/8, 8/13, 13/21 … They match the Fibonacci sequence. In the heads of sunflowers these angles produce two series of curves, one winding clockwise and the other anticlockwise. The specific fraction depends on the time lapse between the appearances of each seed.

When someone custom-designs the core of their soul map, many people choose a flower whose structure becomes the core of their design. You have to wonder if your intuition is responding to Mother Nature and choosing the design optimal for your personal growth.

Finding Your Soul Family is a personal development tool to help you achieve your optimum growth. It contains a number of techniques for you to experiment with, but the overall aim is to increase your consciousness awareness of yourself, your Soul Family and the Life Lessons you are learning. It is these Life Lessons which enable your personal growth.

However, while there are lessons to be recognised and learnt, life is for enjoying. The greatest gift a child can give their parents is to be happy. Have fun building your soul map. Take your time, play with it, reflect and think about the visual picture of your soul map and make any changes that feel right. Above all, make the process your own. Do not be afraid to change the approach, the picture, the colours or other features. I have described how I have seen the process work for my students, but we are all individuals; do the steps that suit you.

Like all personal development, this process will take some time. If all the information came to you on Day 1, you would not have the time to think about it, assimilate it and reflect on what it means to you and your family. Like a building, you cannot put the roof on before you have built the foundation and walls. The building of your soul map is your foundation, and it provides a roadmap for your development. Like a building foundation, your family may not always be visible, but it is the basis of your strength.

Constructing your soul map brings into your conscious awareness all of your Soul Family members, relationships and lessons. The journey of self-discovery is what is important rather than the actual soul map. Nevertheless, the soul map does serve to remind you of what you have learnt in that journey. You will find that you will learn and remember every facet of your soul map. It will become very personal to you, and you will be able to see it in your mind's eye and be able to draw it from memory. You may have some false starts in constructing your picture, but it's important to remain positive.

Looking back, Andrea recalls that some of her early attempts were very crude and a long way from where she needed to be. All attempts at learning are to be celebrated as they reflect your intent to improve and develop yourself. You will find that wherever your intentions are focused your energy goes, and that your intentions thus turn into reality.

Above all, enjoy building your soul map. This journey is not a race but one of personal development. The aim is to enhance your conscious awareness of yourself and to put yourself back in touch with your 'inner you'. Your 'inner you' will provide you with a personal library of knowledge and wisdom that perhaps you have lost touch with. In this journey there is much to be gained and nothing to be lost. If I were asked,

'What is the one thing that this journey can give me?'

I would reply that it is access to a deep pool of calmness which you can visit at any time of the day or night. There you can gain

Your family is your foundation. They may not always be visible but they are the basis of your strength.

All attempts at learning are to be celebrated.

strength and put today's busy, hectic way of living into perspective.

Gyhldeptis, a Native American goddess, offers calmness to those who ask for it. I leave you with a picture of Mother Nature to remind you to seek your own calmness.

Inner peace comes to those who seek it

Chapter 12: Benefits of Creating and Continuing to Use Your Soul Map

There are great benefits from creating your own soul map. It brings pleasure and a greater understanding of your life and your family as you create it. Personally, I have found that this greater understanding has brought more harmony into my family. As we understand each other and our individual needs better, our behaviour towards one another is more appropriate. And as you colour your soul map, relaxation and calmness arrives and in that calm space you connect with your 'inner you'.

Your soul map is like a wise friend who knows you well and will help you to meditate. There are many techniques available to us to calm the noisy brain to achieve a meditative state. With our busy lives, walking meditations and mindful colouring have become a popular means of relaxation. Soul Art uses these techniques, but soul maps go much further, as they are designed specifically to explore the individual, their family and their friends. In creating a soul map, you look at your relationships and the Life Lessons that you are learning. Using Soul Art, your soul map will be highly personal to you and will connect directly with your deep unconscious self.

Your soul map is like a wise friend who knows you well.

Unlike many self-development tools, there is no need for an intermediary such as a shaman, imam, lama, priest, Zen master or facilitator. Soul Art is about communing with yourself to know yourself better and to improve your level of self-insight and learning. With this insight, your personal development will gain some pace as you realise a challenge in your life is an opportunity being presented for you to learn.

Meditation is a process of self-discovery through opening your inner self and allowing something to express itself that you did not know you possessed. Meditating with your personal soul map, which you have built by accessing your 'inner you', greatly enhances the value gained from meditation. This depth of meditation will allow the layers of conditioning acquired in your life to be peeled away and enable your creative essence to express itself.

The effort and love you put into creating your personalised geometric picture will provide you with a meditation roadmap back to your 'inner you'.

To summarise the benefits of *Finding Your Soul Family,* you will have:

- Commenced looking at your **life to date** and identified where **repeated challenges** are being presented to you. These represent **Life Lessons for you to learn** or practise.
- **Started to understand** the reasons for the challenges. This often results in you **approaching each challenge in a more positive frame of mind.** Challenges are an opportunity to learn rather than you being a victim of misfortune.
- **Gained insight into your life and lessons,** which provides you with the opportunity for enhanced self-development.
- **Discovered a mechanism for achieving calmness** and being able to hear the **voice of your 'inner you'.**

- Used the opportunity to reflect on your soul map to **enhance your relaxation and connection to your 'inner you'**. When you reflect using your soul map you will remember your family's dynamics, your relationships and the lessons you are learning. The calmness you experienced while painting your soul map starts to return. In that calm space you can have a dialogue with your 'inner you' and explore further the dynamics of your life and your family. Great insight and wisdom can be accessed.
- Position your soul map on your desk or in your kitchen or any other place where you are busy and can glance at it during moments of stress. You will start to feel your **calmness return.**

Life Lessons

Life Lessons are your means of learning and improving yourself. If you are able to identify them and work with them your opportunity for accelerated learning is much greater. Keep a Thought Diary, as reviewing it and understanding what is going on in your life is a good means of gaining greater wisdom.

Understanding what is going on in your life is a good means of gaining greater wisdom.

Soul Maps Reflect Your Life Journey

Soul Families are dynamic, as life events affect and change how you and your family feel. Expect over time to feel the urge to build a new soul map. This often happens when there are changes in your life. Andrea has painted the following soul maps, shown in Figure 50. They represent her life journey to date.

The first one Andrea created was while she was in fact-gathering mode and learning about herself and her soul family. It contains many different people, colours, lessons and special relationships. This was a period of learning, and Andrea is a strong, central figure in her soul map. The second soul map reflects a period of change in

Figure 50. Andrea's soul maps.

Andrea's life; one chapter of her life was finishing and another one starting. Daffodils come in the spring and represent new beginnings.

The last soul map represents transformation and is from a period in Andrea's life when she was in transformation at home and at work. Green is a colour for personal growth and unconditional love, joy and inner peace. Yellow is for confidence and self-esteem. I loved this soul map so much that Andrea agreed I could use it as my logo. It has amazed me how many people respond to the signs for transformation in this soul map.

Creating your own soul map brings you insight into your life and therefore the opportunity to transform. Used in reflection or meditation, your calmness is enhanced and the connection to your 'inner you' and your personal wisdom is amplified. The gift of creating and using your own soul map is just perfect for you.

Remember, learning continues for your whole life. You are never too old to learn something new!

Why Should I Construct My Soul Map?

Geometric shapes are inherent in nature, our world, our universe. They are so ingrained in the human psyche that geometric patterns occur in every culture and religion. Constructing your own soul map from deep within you reflects the very essence of your being. When your conscious mind contemplates or meditates on the picture that is your soul map, it acts as a road map to take you back to deep within you where you will find a deeper level of understanding and wisdom.

All of the soul maps I have seen constructed by the 'inner mind' rather than the conscious mind have two key elements; they are both still and dynamic. When you contemplate them the eye tends to be drawn to the centre and then across the whole picture, and at the centre you will find stillness. Yet the soul map is dynamic, as it will have many shapes and colours in it. The soul map you have made is a reflection of you and your life experiences. It will help to move your body from tension to relaxation and your mind from habitual chatter to calmness. Then you will be able to listen to the silence and feel comfortable with it, feel the joy and perceive the wisdom that is available to you.

It is said that a picture paints a thousand words. Pictures and symbols go far deeper than words and connect with a more basic and primal part of you. From here your creative essence can rise. The visual impact of your soul map speaks of you and to you, it will embrace your consciousness to assist you with achieving a deep meditation without distraction.

Your soul map acts as a road map to take you back to deep within you.

Listen to the silence, feel the joy and hear the wisdom.

Part 2

Does Your Consciousness Survive Death?

*Are you an eternal being living a physical life
to enhance learning Life Lessons?*

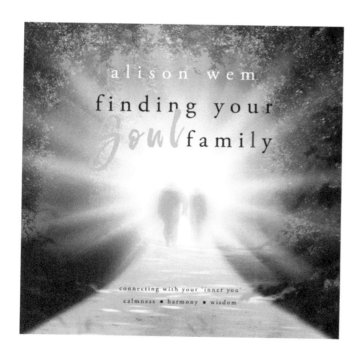

Chapter 13: Mind, Body and Soul

The fact that each of you is made up of a mind, body and soul is not a new concept and is generally accepted. When someone has passed and you look at the body that remains, you know that it is missing something, that important something that made the body the person you knew. You differentiate between each of these elements; mind, body and soul. Yet when you put them together you create the unique person you are.

Since the beginning of time people have sought to understand themselves and their purpose in life. We are all individual, yet part of the whole. Albert Einstein expressed it like this:

A human being is part of the whole, called by us 'universe', a part limited in time and space. He experiences himself, his thoughts and feelings as something separated from the rest – a kind of optical delusion of his consciousness.

Let's look at some of the symbolism and methods people have used throughout history to understand the eternal element of themselves and to connect and consciously be part of the whole. Consider for yourself how this relates to the work you have done in creating your soul map and the experiences you have had communicating with your 'inner you'. It is for you to decide what is appropriate for you, but try to read with an open mind and reserve your judgement until you have read the message.

Chapter 14: Mandalas and Soul Maps

The History of Mandalas

Mandalas are an ancient Eastern art form, originating around the 9th century. Traditional mandalas, often created by Buddhist monks, can be deeply elaborate representations of nirvana. The word 'mandala' is a Sanskrit word meaning 'circle' or 'enclosure'. It was first recorded in the ancient Hindu scripture Rig Veda. However, it is with the Buddhist tradition, in particular Tibetan Buddhism, that mandalas are most commonly associated.

Although mandalas are particularly associated with the East, they have in fact been an important feature of Western traditions as well. In Christianity one of the best-known examples of a mandala is the Celtic Cross. The centre of the cross is also in the centre of the circle. The four arms of the cross represent the four physical dimensions – North, South, East, West – and provide the link between the circle of the heavens and the Earth below. It is thought that the Celtic Cross predates Christianity and was adopted by early Christianity before Roman Christianity became more dominant and introduced the cross of Christ. The halo that surrounds the head of Christ and the saints in Christian art is also an echo of the mandala circle.

Figure 51. Chenrezig sand mandala created at the House of Commons in London when the Dalai Lama visited in May 2008.

In Islam, the illustration of Allah or Muhammad is forbidden. Geometric shapes thus dominate Islamic sacred art and architecture. A segment of the circle, the crescent, together with the full circle in the form of a star, represents the divine in Islam. The inverted half-circle, the dome, represents the arch of the heavens and, by forming the roof of the mosque, allows the whole

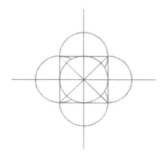

Figure 52. Geometry-based mosque floor plan.

building to become a three-dimensional mandala. The designs of mosques are based on geometric shapes. The central and side domes are based on five circles arranged around a double axis.

Whatever the religious or cultural background, mandalas express through symbolism something that is innate in all of us. Like all true symbols they have arisen from the deep levels of the unconscious mind and serve as a guide which can take us into the mysterious recesses of our own soul.[3]

The Meaning of Mandalas

Derived from Eastern spiritual traditions, mandalas are considered to be maps of the cosmos. Buddhist mandalas are rich with symbolism that can evoke many different aspects of Buddhist teaching. The most basic of mandalas is a circle which symbolizes a path with no beginning and no end. The centre of the circle is a still point in a turning world and is the most sacred of places where one finds tranquillity. Stillness and peace, which are at the core of truth, are

3 For more information about mandalas, see *Mandala Source Book: 150 Mandalas to Help You Find Peace, Awareness and Well-Being*, by David Fontana and Lisa Tenzin-Dolma (London: Watkins, 2014).

always emphasised in a mandala. Although the world is a place of suffering, mandalas are a portal through which we can transcend that suffering. Through such patterns we can attain fulfilment, peace and joy.

In meditation mandalas act as a guide to deeper self-understanding. The diagram represents a sacred or spiritual realm through a pattern of symbolic, geometrically organised shapes and images. In their imagery, the mandalas reflect the macrocosm – the cosmos, and the microcosm – the mind and the body of the individual. They awaken a person's spiritual energy and illuminate their journey. Human consciousness and your 'inner you' respond to man-

Figure 53. Mandala by an anonymous Tibetan painter.

dala patterns whether you believe they do or not. Geometric shapes are multicultural and deeply rooted in the human psyche. Humans respond to the natural order of the universe intuitively, whatever their beliefs.

Mandalas and Meditation

Meditation is a practice for calming the mind. In our busy lives our minds are noisy and in continual chatter, so much so that we do not experience the peaceful tranquil state that is the natural condition of the mind. When asked to be still for a minute many of us find this difficult. Meditation teaches us how to still the mind. Why meditate? You live most of your life in your conscious mind and remain unaware of the depths of your unconscious mind. By helping to still your conscious mind, meditation opens up the depths of your inner self and the wisdom to be found there. Meditation is a path to self-discovery.

Intensely visual, mandalas are symbolic pictures and a powerful tool for use in meditation. They take you on a wordless journey into your mind's deepest mysteries. The step-by-step guidelines in the use of mandalas during meditation that you will use as a beginner can be left behind as you gain confidence and move to an increasingly personal level. Your experience of mandalas is very much your own. The soul map you have created acts as a mandala and is made more personal as you have developed it using your own intuition based on what is right for you. All mandalas at their deepest level are a reflection of self, the cosmos and the love that holds everything together.

Mandalas may be employed for focusing the attention of students, as a spiritual teaching tool and as an aid to meditation. The mandala represents the nature of experience and the intricacies of the mind. The mandala can be regarded as a place separated and protected from the outer world: a place of peace.

In Tibetan Buddhism, the teacher constructs a mandala and gives it to his pupil. The pupil learns every detail of that mandala to the point where they can perfectly construct it without reference to the original. They can recall it in their mind accurately and can use it in meditation. When the pupil is fully intimate with their mandala, they give it back to their teacher to show that they are ready to learn.

The mandala represents what the teacher wants to instruct their pupil in. The whole mandala represents human experience; the circle represents eternity; and the square inside the circle represents the deity that the teacher wants to introduce the pupil to. Typically, there are four gates into the deity, one on each side of the square.

Mandalas take you on a wordless journey into your mind's deepest mysteries.

The mandala is a place separated and protected from the outer world: a place of peace.

Sacred Geometry

Harmony and balance in geometric shapes have been recognised as representing something nonphysical for many thousands of years. As opposed to the routine, mechanical use of geometry in measurement and calculation, Sacred Geometry uses the inherent power of the shape or number. It is a common global heritage seen in the cultures of the Incas, Native American Indians, tribes of Africa, Egyptians, Romans, Asian Indians and Australian Aborigines. Sacred Geometry is seen in sacred rites and structures made by many peoples to represent the celestial on Earth and linking Earth to the heavens.[4]

Soul Art

Soul Art uses Sacred Geometry at the intuitive level in the building of a personal mandala which represents you, your family and friends, your relationships and Life Lessons. Meditating on your personal geometric mandala can take you on a wondrous journey of self-awareness and greater insight which can lead to joy and growing wisdom.

By building your personal mandala using geometric shapes and colours, you can connect with your creativity and enjoy the benefits of using Soul Art as a tool for self-discovery.

Soul Art uses Sacred Geometry at the intuitive level in the building of a personal mandala which represents you and your life.

Andrea and Soul Art

Andrea's soul map is a personal mandala inspired by Tibetan Buddhism, which is where her interests lie. She has chosen shapes and colours that appeal very strongly to her. Andrea has constructed a personal mandala, which she can use in meditation to prepare her

4 For more information, see *How the World Is Made: The Story of Creation According to Sacred Geometry,* by John Michell with Allan Brown (Rochester, VT: Inner Traditions, 2009).

mind for the teaching and self-discovery she is about to embark upon. Understanding that her Soul Family picture was actually a mandala led Andrea to add the outer square to her picture, to represent that the circle was an expression of her life experiences and the inner square now represented the lessons she was studying.

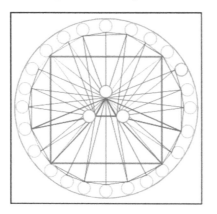 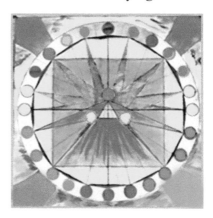

Figure 54. Andrea's design and coloured geometric soul map.

Your soul map may have a different shape or colouring, as you are inspired in a different way to Andrea. However, the concepts behind the geometric mandala and the use of a personalised geometric mandala in reflection or meditation are important for assisting you in your journey of self-discovery and development.

Chapter 15: Does Consciousness Survive Death?

A fundamental question people have asked themselves over the millennia is, 'What happens to me when I die?' All religions attempt to answer this question in their own way. *Finding Your Soul Family* and its associated Soul Art are primarily to do with relationships in this world. However, you might like to consider the possibility that our consciousness survives death. The mind is far more powerful than we usually believe. You have only to speak to friends and family about their loved ones who have passed and whether they have experienced any signals or messages from them and you will be surprised at how many people have. When my father passed my mother was without him for the first time in fifty years. They had a traditional marriage where the men did 'men things' and the women ran the domestic side of their lives together. However, in widowhood my mother amazed herself in the household items she managed to fix. She used to get her husband's tool box out and say, 'Come on, Ron, tell me what I need to do.' The results were truly amazing.

Many Eastern religions believe in reincarnation. Reincarnation is the rebirth of a soul into another body. Christianity, as documented in the early versions of the Bible, once talked about reincarnation,

ഇ൞ര
Consider the possibility
that we are eternal
beings living a life in
a physical body.
ഇ൞ര

121

but over the centuries that concept has been edited out. Ancient civilizations in North America and Africa believe in their ancestors advising the current generation and have rituals which honour their ancestors.

More than half of the world's population has a culture rooted in the belief of reincarnation. They say, 'There is no smoke without fire', and you might like to consider the possibility that we are eternal beings living a life in a physical body. When our body dies perhaps the 'inner you', our deep-seated consciousness, survives with the knowledge of our life experiences, the skills we have learnt and the wisdom we have gained. When born again into another body, the 'inner you' brings that memory bank of knowledge into that body. This knowledge can be accessed when you have learnt the skill to go within, experience the calmness and converse with your 'inner you'.

Consider the alternative: that the skills, knowledge and wisdom gained in one lifetime dissipate on death and are lost. Mother Nature is many things, but in my experience she is always logical and practical. You have only to look at the daffodils and crocuses in the spring. They bloom and die only to bloom again the next spring. Perhaps when a human dies, all is not as it seems.

It is only in relatively recent human history that the modern Western world has challenged the belief in reincarnation. This challenge has shown itself in two ways:

- Refocusing of the belief system in materialism, science and measurement of the world.
- Challenging of religious beliefs and the control that religious institutions exert on the population.

Go within, experience the calmness and converse with your 'Inner You'.

Daffodils bloom and die only to bloom again the next spring.

Modernism, particularly in the Western world, is itself now being challenged. Many people are asserting that there has to be more to life than being born, living a life and dying – game over. In recent years, we have seen an increase in the numbers of Westerners seeking spiritual development and forming spiritual movements. Messages are popularised through songs, for example in the Beatles song 'All We Need Is Love'. The use of drugs is an attempt to speed up the experience of insight without the time-consuming effort of gaining the skill to achieve it naturally. Aldous Huxley describes in *The Doors of Perception* his experience when taking mescaline.

In countries such as Japan and China there are fewer such spiritual groups, as their culture is still more rooted in ancient beliefs. They continue to honour their ancestors and have shrines in their homes to remember them. However, as these cultures become more 'modern' and practise honouring their ancestors less, the need for such groups has increased. At the College of Psychic Studies in London there are increasingly visitors from the East who come to learn and to return to their homelands with the knowledge to assist individuals in their own countries.

In the 1800s there was an increasing quest for truth beyond the sciences. In 1875 the Theosophical Society was founded. Its objectives were:

- To form a nucleus of the universal brotherhood of humanity without distinction of race, creed, sex, caste or colour.
- To encourage the study of comparative religion, philosophy and science.
- To investigate the unexplained laws of nature and the powers latent in Man.

There has to be more to life than being born, living a life and dying – game over.

This quest for truth has continued in the West, with individuals in the last twenty to thirty years becoming well-known for seeking meaning beyond this lifetime, such as Dr Brian Weiss, Doreen Virtue, Deepak Chopra, Dr Wayne Dyer and Eben Alexander. Many of them speak of finding that special place within, where wisdom can be found. The practice of meditation, a technique found in many ancient Eastern religions, is encouraged to help with finding yourself within and connecting to a wider reality. Eben Alexander is a neurosurgeon who wrote of his near-death experience and his experience of the afterlife while in a coma. In his book *The Map of Heaven* he draws on lessons from religious leaders and philosophers as well as scientific investigations into the role of our consciousness. He explores our true place in the universe, what exists beyond death and the journey that all of our souls make.

Human nature has a habit of swinging significantly one way and then another. We have seen this in the swing from religion to modernism. Perhaps there is a more moderate middle path which brings together religion, spiritualism and science. We are just beginning to explore and understand that our consciousness has a part to play in physics and can interact and change the reality of our world as we see it. These discoveries bring science closer to concepts in Eastern religions and spiritualism, concepts which have been accepted for thousands of years.

Ultimately, how a person chooses to behave and to develop as an individual is more the outcome of a conversation with their 'inner you' than a path based on the rules of any particular religion or institution. In many ways, the desire to be a better person and to acquire greater wisdom based on love and compassion is a deeply personal and private conversation. The course of the journey one takes to achieve this goal is immaterial, but undertaking or starting

How a person chooses to behave and develop is a conversation with their "Inner You".

to undertake that journey is hugely important to the individual.

Some seek a facilitator to help them in this journey. Constellation therapy is sometimes undertaken where unresolved historical family trauma still affects the living family. The trauma can originate from events such as murder, suicide, death of a mother in childbirth, early death of a parent or sibling, war, natural disaster, emigration or abuse. Much of Constellation therapy is based on the Zulu culture, a people in southern Africa with whom the founder of Constellation therapy, Bert Hellinger, lived for many years. Unlike Western culture, the traditional Zulu people live and act in a religious world in which the ancestors are the central focal point. The ancestors are regarded as positive, constructive and creative presences. Constellation therapy adopts this belief and, using a facilitator, workshops the dynamics of a family's ancestors to bring into consciousness unresolved feelings and emotions. Once brought into consciousness, this knowledge brings understanding and learning to the current generation. In the workshop, representatives of the ancestors use intuition to experience and express the feelings of the ancestors. This connection with ancestors is a central feature of the Constellation process. Like the techniques I outline in *Finding Your Soul Family*, Constellation therapy brings about a better conscious understanding of our family member relationships and Life Lessons, which aids development in the current generation.

Jill Purce, based in London, believes that if we can all learn to use our voices again, we can re-enchant the world and create harmonious families and communities. Jill specialises in overtone chanting and rituals used in Mongolia and Tibet and among the Native American Indians. Many of the rituals Jill uses are based on shamanism, a practice that involves a practitioner reaching altered states of consciousness in order to perceive and interact with universal energy

Much of Constellation therapy is based on the Zulu culture, a tribe in southern Africa.

and channel it into this world. Jill runs workshops which address family healing using shamanic ceremonies. Andrea was exploring her soul map and decided to attend one of these workshops to see if she could learn more about her ancestors. She participated in a ceremony to honour her ancestors. Andrea recalls:

It was a powerful exercise where I stood at the centre of a circle of individuals representing my ancestors. I said a chant where I honoured each of my ancestors and asked for their blessing. I had a significant conversation with the person representing my mother. This reaffirmed the significance of my mother in my soul map and brought to the surface hidden resentment which dissipated once I understood it.

Both Constellation therapy and Jill Purce's healing voice exercises are aimed at bringing harmony to you and your family by helping you achieve greater understanding of your ancestors through a facilitator or shaman and shamanic practices rooted in ancient civilisations.

Mysticism accepts intuition and the ability to connect with universal energy. Islam speaks of finding the infinite within the small. Science seeks to explain our reality through measurement and maths. These approaches have long been isolated from each other until relatively recent discoveries such as quantum physics and how material behaves at the subatomic level, jumping in and out of our reality. These amazing discoveries demonstrate that there is still much we do not understand about the universe in which we live and grow.

Soul Art transcends religion, mysticism and maths with the use of intuition and connection with your 'inner you', yet uses geometric shapes, a fundamental concept within maths, to build the soul map. I have observed that where various religions have adopted

Andrea honoured each ancestor and asked for their blessing.

Soul Art transcends religion, mysticism and maths with the use of intuition and connection with your 'inner you'.

geometric shapes into their sacred buildings or art, they have attributed the same meaning to the shapes. This makes me wonder if it is as a result of the architect or artist using their unconscious mind in their work, leading to the use of a common language or consciousness regardless of culture or religion.

Your soul map is a picture of your eternal family built using intuition and mathematical symbols. The whole process is about exploring and managing yourself rather than having a third party facilitating your development. There are key differences between Soul Art and shamanic-based development techniques:

1. Soul Art is much simpler than shamanic ritual, as you can do it for yourself without a shaman or facilitator.
2. You can trigger it simply by asking yourself, 'What is it I should do next with my life?'
3. You learn to find that quiet spot within and to listen for the answers to your question, no matter how they choose to arrive.

The techniques are simple, although it takes time and persistence to practice them. Andrea found that as she used Soul Art to explore her relationships and Life Lessons some memories of skills learnt in previous lives came into her mind. Once the life was remembered, she did not forget it again. Andrea did not know how she did it, it just happened – usually in response to a question she asked like, 'Why did that challenge arrive? What am I trying to learn?' or 'Why did that person behave towards me like they did? Is there learning for me in this interaction?' Over time she built up a better understanding of not only lessons she had learnt in previous lifetimes but also lessons she had failed to learn and therefore were tasks she brought into this life. Andrea assumed that remembering earlier lives happened when she was ready in her personal development to access

Soul Art techniques are simple, although it takes time and persistence to practise them.

these memories and accept the invaluable insight they brought.

The library of experience and wisdom gleaned from our former lives is available to us, but it often takes the focus involved in working on something like construction of a soul map to enable us access to it. If you do not find yourself remembering former lives, do not worry. It is just not the right time for you to remember yet. Be reassured that the insight and value that assists your personal development can all be achieved using information from your current life. So do not force trying to remember former lives or give up on your soul map if it does not happen. You will receive the information you need for where you are in your development.

Soul Art and building your soul map are great for modern day living to limit stress and anxiety. It is increasingly important in this always-connected world of mobile phones and email to switch off from the everyday stresses and troubles in the world. Support structures and coping mechanisms are key to preserving and enhancing our health and well-being.

You continue to develop as a person throughout your lifespan, to the moment you take your last breath. When my dad realised he was terminally ill, he had a burst of activity in getting the practical things sorted to help his family when he was no longer here. He changed his car for one he thought my mum would find easier to drive, had a new central heating boiler installed, arranged his own funeral and even ordered flowers to be delivered to my mum for her birthday – a date sadly he did not believe he would reach. Once all of the practical things were done, his focus moved inwards, thinking about who he was and what was going to happen to him. He did not believe in an afterlife. One evening, my dad, mum and I had a deep conversation about consciousness surviving death. My mum, who was not usually very forthright, was very outspoken in

Soul Art is great for
modern day living,
helping to limit
stress and anxiety.

her belief of life after death. Dad did not share her conviction and thought it was only human to desire this to be the case as he neared the end of his life. On the last day of his life, my mum, brother and I held his hand while he learnt his last lesson in this life. It is not easy to watch someone you love take their last breath, but in the last few moments Dad smiled such a big smile. My dad had been anxious about what he would face on death, but that smile made me think that you do not step out of this life into oblivion, as he had feared. Whatever it is, my dad was pleased. I believe his Soul Family had come to guide him home.

'Does our consciousness survive death?' This is really a question you need to answer for yourself. In developing as an individual and trying to practise love and compassion, the answer will come to you.

At the end of the day, the universe is the universe and will continue to function in its own way regardless of our understanding of it. The sun rises each day and sets each evening. It is only in relatively recent history that we have understood that the world is round and rotates while it orbits around the Sun. When Christopher Columbus set out on his voyages in the 1500s, his sailors thought the world was flat and they feared they would fall off the edge if they sailed too far west from Portugal. How our human understanding of the world has changed, yet the universe remains unaltered!

Our understanding of the world has changed, but the universe remains unaltered.

Chapter 16: Life Lessons

Our individual Life Lessons do not come to us all neatly catalogued. We must endeavour to understand what they are so we can modify how we handle a challenge to gain a better probability of learning the lesson. Having an awareness of the types of Life Lessons we address might help you in this process. In this chapter I share the types of Life Lessons I have witnessed my students grappling with in the hope that these examples will assist you with yours.

Themes to Life Lessons

When I looked at my notes from interviews with students and reviewed the lessons they were learning, what jumped out at me was a repeated message that love is always with us and around us. We are not separate individuals, as perhaps we are taught, but very much connected with each other and the universe. I also saw clear messages about how the skills we learn in one life can be used in another life. Although we might not explicitly remember learning a particular skill in a previous life or believe in reincarnation, I strongly believe that we will have a natural aptitude for certain tasks when using those skills again in another life. I believe that we are not all born equal, because we bring with us our previous learning.

We are not separate individuals, as perhaps we are taught, but very much connected with one another.

I wonder whether these are general messages we all need to learn. The overarching lesson for me as I read through notes from my discussions with students was that there is purpose to being born and experiencing a life.

As you spend time with your soul map, meditating on it and receiving wisdom, you will find messages in the lessons specifically for your development. Perhaps your lesson is that you are trying to practise good communication and to appreciate the value good communication can bring. You may have a love of art, music or architecture, which could be the product of previous experiences. Analyse what you are good at, what passions you have and what repeated challenges you encounter. What you learn from this analysis will tell you the skills and loves you have brought into this life, along with the lessons you may have yet to learn.

Many of the challenges in our lives are not just bad luck but situations we have in a sense asked for to help us learn a lesson. How you tackle a challenge is as important – if not more important – than what you achieve by overcoming the challenge. Life is rather like a role play you do to improve skills. That is why, if you do not get it right, you will see the same type of challenge appearing repeatedly until you finally learn the lesson.

A conscious awareness of the lessons you are learning will speed up the rate at which you learn them. When the same challenge presents itself to you in the future, you will recognise it as an opportunity to learn your lesson and perhaps approach it with more care and a different attitude.

I have found that lessons can generally be grouped into categories. See how the lessons that you have learned or the ones that you are still learning relate to these categories:

There is purpose to being born and experiencing a life.

- Love and loving
- Connection with others
- Connection with universal energy through emotions
- Retaining skills across our lives
- Working and living with compassion
- Guidance in learning our lessons

Do not limit yourself to these categories; you may have some additional ones. By way of an example, below are the most common lessons which students share of having learnt or are learning. Some of them may resonate with you. You will have other, different, lessons that you are learning. Analyse your Thought Diary and soul map to identify and group your lessons.

Analyse your Thought Diary and soul map to identify and group lessons.

Love and Loving

Scattered throughout your life will be lessons in being loved and loving others. Students' messages relating to love are these:

- *I remember with love knowledge that was imparted to me with love.*
- *I love someone for who they are, not what they are.*
- *Sometimes it's difficult to show someone that I love them and want to please them.*
- *It is important for me to trust the people I love.*
- *It is important to learn to love yourself and be kind to yourself.*
- *The love and promises I give and receive in this life will be remembered across lives.*

Connection with Others

Western religions teach us that upon death you go to heaven or hell. They do not have the concept of karma and reincarnation. It is interesting to note that the very earliest versions of the Christian

Bible did contain the concept of reincarnation, but it was edited out over time by church leaders.

I grew up in a Western culture, so I found it difficult to accept that we are eternal beings constrained in a physical body. Once I had accepted this idea through experience and observation, I much preferred the idea that the eternal being is very much connected to others in the universe.

When people talk about this topic it never ceases to surprise me how many people have had personal experiences of communication with loved ones still living or who have passed. This communication may occur through smells and their associations, sounds, assistance with a task you could not have done on your own, or an object being moved. It is not always conventional words that form the communication. Talk to your friends and family to see if they have experienced communications with loved ones who have passed, or perhaps if there is someone you know who has the ability to connect with the universal energy and heal others, for example, using reiki, ask them about their experiences. Reiki is a therapy often described as palm or hands-on-body healing. You'll find a fuller description of reiki in the Glossary.

Here are some students' messages relating to being connected to others:

- *I am never really alone.*
- *I always have loved ones around me – I just might not recognise them.*
- *In loneliness and grief I can find an inner strength.*
- *Friendship is important to me.*
- *I take with me into each life the essential character of my soul.*

Connection with Universal Energy Through Emotions

Emotions are a very strong and tangible energy which you can both give out and receive. If you are not sure that this is so, think of a time when your mother was either cross or disapproving of you. I'll bet you could feel her annoyance without her even opening her mouth. My family says that when I am cross the air seems to crackle around me. We as individuals and our emotions are not islands. Others can feel our emotions.

Hope and intention are powerful emotions in moving your life forward. In his book *Man's Search for Meaning,* Viktor E. Frankl describes his experiences as a Jew in an extermination camp during World War II. Hope was so significant to survival: A person with hope was far more likely to survive, even if they were physically weak. This book is a remarkable tribute to hope and the positive effects of retaining your dignity and compassion even in the most tragic of circumstances.

Emotions connect us with our companions and with the wider universal energy. Increasingly there is recognition that the energy you send out comes back to you. If you send out anger, angry people and situations will come back to you. Likewise, if you send out love and compassion, they will come back. So, as the saying goes, 'Be careful what you wish for.' There are many good books on these laws of attraction, a topic well worth reading about.

Many of us have lessons to learn about managing our emotions. We need to allow ourselves to feel our emotions, but we need to acknowledge and accept them and then let them go so that they do not become destructive.

Here are some students' messages relating to connection with our emotions and the universal energy:

Our emotions are not islands. Others can feel our emotions.

Hope and intention are powerful emotions in moving your life forward.

- *I must remember to share my journey of discovery with others to encourage them to join me.*
- *I have successfully learnt how to connect with the inner me and universal energy before.*
- *My questions are usually answered over time.*
- *My life should be balanced with both family life and personal development.*
- *I can have both family and a spiritual life.*
- *My guides have a personality and sense of humour.[5]*
- *This time I awaken from a 5,000-year slumber to remember who I am.*

Retaining Skills Across Our Lives

When she practised Soul Art, Andrea initially discovered more about herself in her current life and family. Then quite unexpectedly when she asked a question, she was reminded by way of encouragement of a life skill learnt before this life which could help her in her current situation – knowledge which made the challenge she faced seem less daunting. As I analysed Andrea's innate skills and the lessons she is learning, it seemed to me that both the skills and the bad habits she learns in one life she takes with her into subsequent lives.

If we have not perfected a skill, we will continue to get opportunities to practise and improve.

If we have not perfected a skill, we will continue to get opportunities to practise and improve it. Once we have demonstrated that we can use this skill well the opportunities diminish.

It is important to understand that you do not have to remember previous lives to recognise and analyse repeated opportunities which arrive in your life for learning – for example, improving communications, managing anger or having belief in oneself. Reflection on your current life is sufficient to recognise your strengths and potential lessons.

---

5 **Guide.** A person in the spirit world who guides and protects you. Guides in this world would be parents, teachers and mentors.

Here are some students' messages relating to skills we retain across our lives:

- *Communicating my feelings in the right manner at the right time is important.*
- *Working together with others providing them with my support and receiving their support in return is good.*
- *Working as part of a team I am stronger than I am on my own.*
- *Focus, concentration and practice enable me to achieve amazing things.*
- *Skills learnt in a previous life can be reused in my current life.*

Working and Living with Compassion

Life Lessons are personal to you and where you are in your development. You will have your own set of lessons. By sharing students' lessons I hope you will come to understand that they are lessons in love and compassion and do not relate to building empires or making money. No matter what your life path is, these lessons are relevant to us all. Specific lessons about working and living with others have included these:

- *I must communicate well and openly to maintain good relationships with others.*
- *I choose my words carefully and with consideration.*
- *Sometimes I should remain silent as my views are not desired.*
- *I must learn not to dictate and be too pushy and to give people time to assimilate my message.*
- *I need to allow other people to make their own decisions about their lives.*
- *I must continually practise good communication to improve human interaction.*
- *I can build a new life even from very difficult circumstances.*

Life Lessons teach us about love and compassion and do not relate to building an empire or making money.

- *I must be receptive to change to assess what feels right and to adopt the good elements.*
- *Beautiful buildings can provide me with a space of peace and harmony.*

Guidance on Learning Our Lessons

This was by far the longest list of messages. It made me realise that families here in the physical world and our eternal families are much the same. Older, wiser members of the family are always trying to guide the younger, developing members of the family. Here are some students' messages relating to guidance on how to learn our lessons:

- *My life is for living and enjoying. Joy is good.*
- *Working through a challenge I face is often more rewarding than walking away from it.*
- *There is often a lesson for me to learn in tragic events that I experience.*
- *Whatever I miss or do not get right in this life, I will get a chance to try again in another life.*
- *Challenges often help me to learn a lesson about what I will allow to happen to me.*
- *It is important to be flexible in life and embrace the challenges it throws at me.*
- *I might believe that I have learned a lesson, but I will likely check in a later life if this is true.*
- *A lesson learnt transcends the lives I lead.*
- *Reactions and emotions in my life which may seem irrational can be rooted in experiences from previous lives.*
- *Experiences in one life can create anxieties in another.*
- *When my behaviours in this life shock or baffle me, they might relate back to a previous life.*

- *I do not always remember the full detail of a life, but I may remember cultures, places, trades, etc.*
- *The hurt and anger at the pointless loss of my son in a previous life resurfaced in this life with great ferocity. It was only because I challenged why this anger was so strong that I learnt of the previous life.*
- *All of my attempts to improve myself and my life are good and should be encouraged.*

Although these lessons relate to my students, most of them are good pointers to anyone wishing to enhance their personal development as a human being.

A lesson learnt transcends the lives we lead.

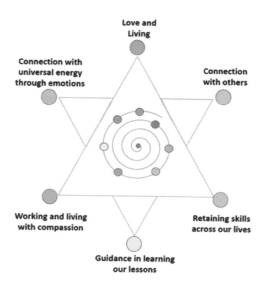

Figure 55. Life Lessons theme chart.

Chapter 17: Taking Responsibility for Your Own Life

There can be many reasons for seeking personal development. In my case it was a result of being driven to the extremes of life through widowhood and feeling unable to cope. You may simply feel something is missing in your life and are seeking a better way of living, or you may be looking for greater balance between your job and home or in the manner in which a key relationship within your life is working. Whatever the reason, many seek a sense of completion, wholeness or oneness to help them live a happier life.

It is good to have a vision of how you would like your life to look, feel and be. It may take courage to start this journey and some effort to get going, but once you are on the journey it will gain its own momentum. Think of a swan taking flight. There is much wing-flapping and effort, but its body slowly rises so its feet are paddling across the water. Eventually the swan is airborne and tuck its feet up underneath its body. Then it becomes the beautiful swan again with a slower but steady beat of its wings. Taking responsibility for your own life and growth path is much the same.

You may be asking yourself: *'What is the purpose of my life?'*

Many seek a sense of completion, a wholeness or oneness to live a happier life.

Lives are made of relationships with other people. Improving the quality of these relationships will improve the quality of your life. In my view, the simplest answer to this age-old question is that life is for enjoying. Sometimes people just need to give themselves permission to enjoy their life. However, the journey of life is never without its challenges, which are opportunities to learn and grow. I believe that maintaining a positive mindset as you tackle these challenges makes the learning easier. You become the pupil in learning wisdom rather than the victim of a challenging situation. This is sometimes easier said than done, but it is worth remembering. It is what I lost sight of in the early days of widowhood.

Widowhood taught me some hard lessons on taking responsibility for my own well-being and creating a life I could enjoy rather than just endure. Widowhood is different from divorce. You are physically separated from your partner while you still love them, and you go on loving them after they have passed. You are alone and they are not there to consult on important things such as the welfare of the children. For nearly two years I struggled with this dilemma. To the world it looked like I had 'moved on'. I cared for my children and got them to school. Their friends were frequently in our home and my children had a good social life. It was very different for me. My heart was a desert, and I felt so dreadfully alone. I was even losing my identity and becoming known as 'Jamie's Mum' rather than Alison.

I still woke up at 2 a.m. each morning unable to get back to sleep. For twenty-four years I had slept with my husband, and now our bed seemed so empty and the covers so heavy without him. I can honestly say that I functioned in the world but I was not alive. The first thing I finally managed to do for me was to go to reiki and receive some healing. Many years later the reiki master told me that

Widowhood taught me some hard lessons on taking responsibility for my own well-being.

when I turned up the first time, she could see and feel my heart in two pieces. The reiki master encouraged me to meditate and to read widely in spiritual books. The combination of these two activities were a positive step forward for me taking responsibility for my own life, and I started to sleep most of the night. Once I went to the place where you go when you sleep and drank from the Cup of Life, my well-being, although not fixed, was much improved.

On the night that my husband passed I fell out of the Married Club. I had no singleton friends, and while my married friends invited me into their homes, I felt out of place. Of course I continued to meet with my girlfriends, but I missed the balanced energy of mixed company. I wanted my identity back, and I wanted a life I could enjoy.

In desperation I decided to create a Widow/Widowers Club. I had not had the courage to entertain as a singleton before, but I gave a dinner party for eight people. My approach was simple – singletons had to be either a widow or a widower and couples had to have at least one partner who had experienced being a widow/widower. I was amazed I attracted so many people to my soiree. With my courage pinned to my chest, the evening kicked off – and we had so much fun. Laughter had returned to my home and my life to ease my hurting heart.

From that evening I was invited to other dinners, and we started to go to parties as a group. We made sure no-one was left out and that everyone danced! Several months later, I met the man who is now my husband, and as the saying goes the rest is history. However, my husband did say that he had seen me before the night he approached our widows' group to ask me to dance. On that occasion, I had seemed so sad he had not liked to approach me. In that instance, I had perpetuated the life I was trying to move away from.

My own desire and intentions built the life I experienced.

If you seek to improve the relationships in your life, you are heading in the right direction.

My widows' dinner party was a turning point in my life, one where I finally realised that my own desires and intentions built the life I experienced. Enthusiasm and passion are good companions to take with you on this journey called life.

Gaining an understanding of the purpose of your life takes time, but it will be unveiled to you if you desire to know. In my view relationships are the key to life, and if you seek to improve the relationships in your life, you are heading in the right direction. To learn to sustain giving and receiving love in a relationship, long after the initial bloom of romance, is wisdom itself.

Healing yourself is about achieving that sense of wholeness and balance. To achieve this you will need to take responsibility for your own well-being – a lesson I learnt the hard way. Sharing is another good way of practising balance.

Can Anyone Gain Value from *Finding Your Soul Family* Techniques?

Harry, a person dear to me who struggles with substance abuse, said this about *Finding Your Soul Family:*

Your Soul Family by its creative nature is accessible to all, even those struggling with substance abuse. It does reduce connectivity with your 'inner you', but never blocks it totally. You are never abandoned by your 'inner you', you are always loved. In my view, Your Soul Family can help those in an abusive habit to realise it is a mistake and to build a better life.

Life is a collection of learning experiences through events shared with others. Through those life experiences you choose to share, a two-way process is enacted through giving and receiving. Energy moves backwards and forwards between you and those with whom you are sharing. This is commonly seen in acts of communication, helping others, teaching, guiding, co-operating and discussion. It is these acts which are needed for our survival and are critical for our development.

When giving and receiving does not happen in a balanced way, you see argument, disease and war. Balanced acts of sharing are important for both your physical and mental health. Sharing has a positive impact for both the giver and the receiver. The symbol for sharing appears in many cultures, but perhaps the most well-known is the interlacing of Yin and Yang or male and female energy.

Balanced acts of sharing are important for both your physical and mental health.

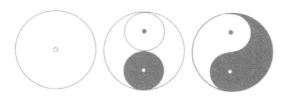

Figure 56. Energy pictures.

Development of balanced energy pictures is based on geometric shapes, which are such a fundamental element of our universe. Many of our Life Lessons are about improving communication and interaction with another person. Where a person repeatedly gives of themselves, they can become out of balance and need to learn to receive. Taken to an extreme the person can make themselves ill. Many cultures exonerate inappropriate giving, such as Robin Hood, who stole from the rich to give to the poor, but to be healthy giving needs to be true and balanced. Taking time to educate someone to do the right thing would have been a better way of giving.

Life is meant to be lived and enjoyed. Dreams are meant to be followed. You might not get there in one step, but even little steps towards your dream are satisfying and worthwhile. *The Alchemist* by Paulo Coelho is a fable about following your dream, and it brings into focus the importance of doing what is really important to you rather than what other people want you to do.

Finding Your Soul Family is not a shortcut, a quick fix or a formula for a happier life. Instead, it guides you in honestly looking at the essence of who you are and your life so far. It looks at the force behind your birth and the Life Lessons you want to master, along with those you have already mastered. Finding your Soul Family is a simple process but one not so easy to accomplish. It is easy and enjoyable to create your first soul map, which brings your first set of insights, but nobody is going to remind you to continue to practise reflecting on your soul map or to maintain your Thought Diary to strengthen your communication with your 'inner you'. You will need to take responsibility for increasing your conscious awareness and to show self-initiative to cultivate the skill to communicate with your 'inner you'. This is a new experience and not everybody is ready for such a responsibility. I am grateful you are reading this book and exploring how you might make your life more complete and in balance.

Cross Roads by W. M. Paul Young tells the tale of a multimillion-aire whose life is lacking in family, love and healthy relationships. It speaks to all of us who have got things wrong in life and would like to put them right. We all have challenges in our lives, but the essence of who you are is how you handle those challenges. You might wonder why you became sick or have such an awful manager and expect others to fix you or your situation. When you go inwards, you realise that you can be the cause of your happiness, health and good relationships. Many are still learning to take this responsibility for themselves. The techniques in *Finding Your Soul Family* can assist you, in an enjoyable manner, to take that responsibility. You can expect to feel the desire over time to create many soul maps. Each one will represent your life in a moment of time. Typically, the first soul map is about getting to know who is in your family, while the following ones seem to guide you when you are entering another phase of your learning and growth. I would consider it a privilege to have helped provide you with some of the tools for your learning.

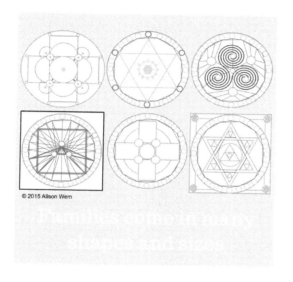

© 2015 Alison Wem

Chapter 18: After I Have Built
My Soul Map, What Next?

Creating your soul map reawakens the communications between your conscious mind and your 'inner you'. Your 'inner you' will be keen to send you insight so you have the opportunity to access your personal wisdom. To maximise the benefit from this connection, I would encourage you to:

1. **Continue to keep a Thought Diary.** You often receive insight as you wake up, in the shower and going to sleep. If you do not note down your thoughts you will know you have had an insight but not be able to remember what it was! This can be very frustrating. At times of high activity, such as after creating a new soul map, I keep a Post-it note pad by my bed and in the bathroom. As insight comes I quickly make a note and later stick it in my Thought Diary. It gives me great pleasure to reread them and to achieve a greater understanding of myself and my family.

2. **Review your soul map and continue to revise it.**

3. **Paint another soul map** to include your revisions.

4. **Join the Your Soul Family community.** The home of our international community is at www.yoursoulfamily.com with articles

on mindfulness at home and at work, comments and feedback, downloads of the templates, and Early Bird alerts of new publications.

5. For those of you in the UK, consider:

    - **Attending a workshop** in London, where we do a number of exercises to tease out what you know about yourself and your family to enrich the meaning in your soul map.
    - **Hosting a Your Soul Family workshop for your friends.** With four paying guests, you go free. I am prepared to travel out of London.
    - Attending **my regular evening course** in London, where you will learn to communicate with your 'inner you' to receive life guidance.
    - **Individual coaching sessions,** which are available over Skype or face-to-face in London.

    Check www.yoursoulfamily.com for the latest programme of events.

6. For those of you outside the UK, there are now some events in Europe. Plus, this book is aimed at providing you with many of the exercises I use in my workshops. If you have any questions, please contact me through the website. Individual coaching sessions are available over Skype. Over time I am planning to create online courses. Watch for their releases or ask for an Early Bird alert at www.yoursoulfamily.com.

7. There is a building community on mindfulness from people trying to bring it into their lives in work and at home. Each of you is one person whether you are at home or work and should try to maintain your calmness and connection to your 'inner you' in both arenas.

Stay in touch with the Your Soul Family community:

www.yoursoulfamily.com

Thank you for joining the Your Soul family team. Enjoyed *Finding Your Soul Family*? Here is what you can do next. If you have loved the book and have a moment to spare, I would really appreciate a short review. Your help in spreading the word is gratefully received.

I wish you well in creating your soul map and on your journey of self-discovery to the heart of your eternal Soul Family and comprehending the Life Lessons you are learning together. You will have started to understand who you are and where you are going. May your ongoing journey be both productive and enjoyable. As some say: *'To stand on the brink of what is coming feeling eager, optimistic anticipation – with no feeling of impatience, doubt, or unworthiness hindering the receiving – that is life at its best.'*

If you have any questions, please contact me through the Your Soul Family website, www.yoursoulfamily.com.

Love,
Alison Wem

Epilogue

The ideas in this book have come from my 'inner you' as I have learnt to access my inner knowing and the library of wisdom and knowledge learnt from experiencing numerous lives. While the techniques in *Finding Your Soul Family* will work looking only at your current life, the insight is much greater and deeper if you go beyond this life.

Many find this journey of self-discovery remarkable, taking them beyond this life to other lives they have lived. In these other lives they recognise people from their current family and friendship group and come to realise that their Soul Family accompanies them as they develop and grow. Comfort is often found in this knowledge, along with the assurance that if you got something wrong in this life you will have a chance to get it right in another life.

You now understand Soul Family and Soul Art along with how to use these concepts as an aid to your personal growth. Here are some anecdotes about my experience of using it.

Building my soul maps has put me back in touch with my 'inner you'. The insight and wisdom I found within myself has brought more understanding to my extended family and therefore more harmony than would otherwise have been possible. I identified family and friends with whom I have repeatedly shared lives. The

Self-discovery can take you beyond this life to other lives you have lived.

knowledge that they would repeatedly share in my lives and help me with my lessons I found comforting, as Western teaching asserts that we are largely alone. This wisdom of how the universe works brought balance to my well-being.

Intuitively, I knew that reincarnation existed from the first time I read about it when I was in my twenties. Now I wholeheartedly believe it to be true. When I first spoke about it, people asked me what was the basis for my belief in reincarnation. The answer is very simple: I can remember a number of lives. I do not remember the whole life in detail, down to what I ate for dinner. Rather, I remember important moments in my previous lives which are relevant learning points for something in my current life. My memory bank of lives acts like a teaching tool in this life.

The process of building your soul map is one of enhancing your self-awareness. The value is in the journey rather than the end result, so expect it to take some time. This is not always as simple as it sounds in this world, where achieving a tangible goal is so highly valued. Even as I struggle to put the right things into this book, I see my guide lying on my sofa with his head resting on the back of it and his legs stretched out in front of him, chuckling and saying, 'Relax. The right things will come to you. Don't rush it.' Then I see his chum Chen leaning over my computer putting lots of energy into my files and doing all the work. Nice one!

In case this viewpoint is entirely new to you, I will outline an example of the process I experience when remembering a past life:

- **Trigger.** I am exploring the use of sound to enhance my connection with universal energy.
- **Focused attention.** I attended a lecture by Jill Purce on chanting. She is leading us in a chant and we feel very connected to each other and our inner selves.

ಌಌ
I remember important moments in my previous lives which are relevant learning points for my current life.
ಌಌ

- **A simple, clear question.** Chanting is interesting and I definitely felt more connected, but when has chanting been important to me in a life experience?
- **Answer retrieval.** The inner me quickly reviews my lives and gives me a memory of being a North American black slave working in a gang lifting and shifting heavy items. I'm given a scene and the gang is chanting. No more detailed information.
- **Wait for detail.** I thank the inner me and let the question be. I wait one to two weeks and think of the slave gang a couple of times but nothing more.
- **Detail arrives.** I now have a knowing of that life and scene and am able to write the following paragraph plus see the scene and feel how I felt at that time. I sense and know the scene but do not experience the actual pain of that life. If it does start to arrive, I promptly state that this is a memory and not pain to be experienced in this life. It promptly withdraws.

Experiment with triggers and find ones that work for you.

Experiment with triggers and find ones that work for you. My triggers have included receiving universal energy through reiki, visiting countries and cultures I have lived in before, looking at stones I picked up in countries where I had lived lives important to me and sitting in a psychic development circle.

- **Analyse the life for lessons.** I took two lessons from this life memory: chanting does magnify the link with our companions and the inner you; and when help is asked for it can arrive in unexpected ways.
- **Record the detail.** I noted the life detail and lessons in my Thought Diary to make sure I would not forget them.

I am a black Virginian, a North American slave working in a gang assisting in the construction of large buildings and possibly ships. The gang has to life heavy wooden logs and planks, carry them to the right place in the building and then place them into position. There is no skill in this work. We are just providing the muscle power to lift and shift. We are cheap labour doing much of what machinery would be used to do today. The work is long, hard and boring. My life is one of hard labour and endurance. When I stand in line with my gang, the man in front of me has a strong and beautiful body, much like a weightlifter today. His smooth black skin shines with the glisten of sweat from his labour. His arms are thick and muscular, his back broad and strong. By comparison I feel puny and wish for some help. My arms ache and my back hurts. I find it challenging work physically. The foreman of our gang uses chanting to synchronise our efforts – lift, shift, shift, shift, place. We turn the instructions into a song and chant. The chanting brings benefits I am not expecting. Engaging with the song and hearing my own voice lifts the boredom of the task, moves my thoughts away from the pain in my body and eases the pain, the labour becomes bearable as I tap into some unknown energy. I no longer feel so puny.

In the process outlined it seems as if the initial trigger – the focus and question – enables the inner me to run down the corridors of my library of memories. I access the index of memories and read the headlines. However, it takes longer for me to read the detail of the memory, so it takes time for it to arrive. The awareness can arrive in many ways: feelings, knowing and heightened awareness of objects, words or pictures around me. This link to my inner memories is tenuous and can easily be lost. I have found that writing it down strengthens the link and prevents it being broken.

If you decide to try out this process, do make sure that you keep the question simple. It does not work very well for complex questions. Once again, do remember that not everyone can remember past lives. No-one is saying you must remember past lives, and you should not try to force it. The information will come to you when you are ready to receive it. Even if you do not consciously remember past lives, it does not mean you do not access skills and wisdom you gained in a past life. Much as when a baby cries for attention, it is a natural reflex and just happens. Likewise, if you request access to your personal wisdom, it will just happen.

I wish you well in reading your personal library of wisdom.

ಬಂದ
Past life information
will come to you
when you are ready
to receive it.
ಬಂದ

calmness-harmony-wisdom

Frequently Asked Questions

How fast should I progress through the techniques?

There is no easy answer to this question. You should go through them at the pace with which you feel comfortable. However, I recommend that before you start you look through the book to understand what is involved and what you are trying to achieve. The text callout boxes highlight some key points to facilitate your overview. When you have a broad understanding you can then go through the book, following the steps to create your soul map.

I feel stuck. What should I do?

Most people find that their development comes in bursts. If you feel that you are not getting any new insight at the moment, just enjoy your soul map. Leave it where you can see it and remember the insight you have gained so far. Enjoy feeling the calmness return when you look at it and pass any worries you have to your 'inner you' to lighten your load. Alternatively, put your soul map away for a while and take it out again when you feel ready to do some more work on it. You may be surprised at how many changes you might want to make to it when you take it out again.

If you are asking a question, make sure it is simple. Otherwise the answer can be confusing, leading you to think there is no insight arriving. When you are ready to receive some information, it will arrive. Just make sure you are open to receiving it. Remember that messages arrive in all sorts of ways – a knowing, words in a book jumping out at you, a message in a song on the radio that resonates with you, a billboard in the street that has a sentiment that brings the answer to your question. You have to be alert to receive your message.

Do I need to do Your Soul Family exclusively and nothing else?

Trying out different techniques for your personal development is good, as you will resonate more strongly with some rather than others. But though variety is good, do try not to overwhelm yourself. For each approach, do give it enough time and energy so that you gain the benefit from what it has to offer you. There is a danger of doing too many approaches at the same time, in that you may flit from one to another and not achieve the progress you are seeking. Just monitor yourself and make sure you are not putting yourself under too much pressure.

Where can I get any new templates?

Periodically, Your Soul Family will publish new templates. Go to our website for the most up-to-date posts at www.yoursoulfamily.com. Alternatively, if you desire a new soul map, have you considered designing one of your own? Chapter 8 of this book provides you with guidance in producing your own custom design.

No more insight is coming to me at the moment. Is this normal?

You will receive the information you need for where you are in your life right now. Just make sure you can find that calm space by stopping the noisy chatter of your mind. You can do this by meditation or by reflecting on your soul map. In that calm space you will be able to hear your 'inner you'. Your 'inner you' may not be providing new insight but will always be offering you love and assurance. This is good in itself and not to be dismissed.

Do I have to believe in past lives for Your Soul Family to work?

No belief in past lives is needed to enable the techniques in Your Soul Family to work. All the information you need to build your soul map and to receive insight on who you are and where you are going can be found from the facts in your life today. The nature of the relationships in your life and the Life Lessons you want to learn can all be determined by who you are today. Just having a better conscious appreciation of your Life Lessons can enhance your rate of development.

Does my energy colour reflect my soul development?

Chakras are energy centres in your body. There are seven key chakras running through the centre of your body. Each has its own colour – red, orange, yellow, green, blue, indigo, mauve. Each is also associated with an organ and a set of emotions. If you are to feel complete, each of the chakras needs to be working well and in balance with one another. I believe your loved ones in your Soul Family talk to you using the energy from one of their chakras as it emphasises the nature of the communication they have with you. See the Glossary for more information on chakras and their meanings.

Some people do believe that the energy colour used by a soul also reflects their level of development. Michael Newton in his books *Journey of Souls* and *Destiny of Souls* discusses the life we lead between our lives, soul energy colour, soul groups and our development. He has obtained this information as a therapist undertaking hypnosis regression with his clients. He found that through life regression they could go back to before they were born into past lives and sometimes the time spent between lives. These books are well worth the read and you can draw your own conclusion.

What does it mean if I get very negative or frightening thoughts or messages?

It usually means your mind is trying to take control. This can happen when you relax and start to communicate with your 'inner you'. Your mind wants control and can come up with all manner of things to interrupt the communication. If this happens, stop doing Your Soul Family, repeat several times that this information is not for you and close down.[6]

---

6 *Closing down.* As you work with Your Soul Family your energy has opened so you can communicate more easily with your 'inner you'. Closing down protects you from being overly sensitive to others' emotions and thoughts. See the Glossary for more information on how to close down.

Acknowledgements

Writing and publishing this book has been a journey in itself. I have not undertaken this journey alone and I would like to thank my family and friends for their assistance.

Thank you, Wang, Henri, Chen, Lu Pen, Akhen, Don, Quentin, Madame Blavatsky, Father Colm, and others for your help and encouragement in writing this guide.

Thank you, Gerrie March, my mentor in this life, who helped me to get to know myself better and encouraged me not to procrastinate in writing this book. Steven Hiatt, who guided me through the maze that is the publishing process.

To my family and friends, in particular David Defty and Nigel Peace, who took the time to read and reread the evolving drafts, thank you for your time and patience.

Finally, a big thank you to my husband for your patience and forbearance when patience does not come easily to you. I spent so much of our precious weekends, when we led busy working lives, with my nose to the computer writing.

Dear Reader,

In writing this guide it is my hope that it will have created some 'hollow ways' to assist you to find your way back to the heart of your eternal Soul Family. To help me to improve the communication of this approach, I would appreciate your feedback on what was interesting and easy to follow and which areas were perhaps less interesting or less well explained and could be improved.

All feedback is welcome. If you have any comments or questions, please email me at Alison.wem@yoursoulfamily.com.

Love, Alison Wem

If you are interested in continuing your journey with ideas from Your Soul Family, follow my blog on www.yoursoulfamily.com *and my Facebook page. Search 'Alison Wem – Your Soul Family'.*

Glossary

Chakras. Originating in Hinduism and Tantric Buddhism, chakras are energy centres in our bodies through which energy flows. There are seven key chakras, which align with our spine up through our bodies. Each has a specific colour and shape and is associated with a specific organ and emotions. It is through our emotions that we speak with the universe and universal energy. Therefore, the emotion associated with a chakra can add meaning to the family member in your soul map with that colour – for example, the yellow members of Andrea's family. Yellow is for confidence, self-worth, self-esteem and being in control of your life. The yellows in Andrea's soul map, in their individual ways, are all supporters of what she is trying to achieve in her life. At moments of self-doubt they are there to help her with her confidence.

> **Root Chakra.** Found at the base of our spine in the tail-bone area. Red in colour, it is our foundation and addresses survival issues such as food and money.
>
> **Sacral Chakra.** Found in the lower abdomen about two inches below the navel. Orange in colour, it is abundance, well-being, pleasure and sexuality.

Solar Plexus Chakra. Found in the upper abdomen in the stomach area. Yellow in colour, it is our ability to be confident and in control of our lives. It gives us our self-worth, self-confidence and self-esteem.

Heart Chakra. Found in the centre of the chest just above our heart. Green in colour, it is our ability to love. It gives us our love, joy and inner peace.

Throat Chakra. Found in the throat. Blue in colour, it gives us our ability to communicate, express our feelings and the truth.

Chakra symbols.

The chakras

Third Eye Chakra. Found in the forehead between the eyes. Indigo in colour, it is our intuition, imagination, wisdom, ability to think and make decisions.

Crown Chakra. Found at the very top of the head. Mauve in colour, it is our connection to spirituality, pure bliss.

Closing Down. As you work with Your Soul Family your energy becomes more open, improving your ability to talk to your 'inner you'. After working on a Your Soul Family exercise and before you get on with your everyday life, it is advisable to 'close down' your energies. Otherwise, as you go out and about you will be very sensitive to people's emotions and thoughts. Closing down is much like you leaving your home – you would not leave the front door wide open for all to enter. After you have finished the Your Soul Family work, close your eyes and imagine a big front door on your chest. Close the door, take a big key and lock the door. Put the key in your pocket and know that you are protected and safe.

Guide. A person in the spirit world who guides and protects us. Everyone has a guide; you just may not recognise them. Often it's the person you chat to in your head who helps you in times of stress or if you are in need of company. I chatted to mine for decades before I knew what or who he was. This amused him as he has a great sense of humour.

Inner You or Higher Self. A term associated with many belief systems, its basic premise describes an eternal, omnipotent, conscious, and intelligent being who is one's real self. The role of the inner you or higher self is to watch over you and help steer you in the direction you intended to go when you created your life plan.

Intuition. Something that one knows or considers likely from instinctive feeling rather than conscious reasoning. There are many synonyms, including hunch, feeling, feeling in one's bones, gut feeling, inkling, sneaking suspicion, suspicion and impression.

Karma. From the philosophy of Hinduism and Buddhism, where the universe runs according to certain laws. In the law of 'cause and effect', karma is the cause of your actions – mental, vocal and physical – which generate an effect. The belief is that whatever you do comes back to you – for example, if you do something good, something good will happen to you, and vice versa.

Mandala. Is a spiritual and ritual symbol representing the universe. Mandalas may be employed for focusing the attention of students, as a spiritual teaching tool and as an aid to meditation. The mandala represents the nature of experience and the intricacies of the mind. The mandala can be regarded as a place separated and protected from the outer world, a place of peace.

In Tibetan Buddhism, the teacher constructs a mandala and gives it to their pupil. The pupil learns every detail of that mandala to the point where they can perfectly construct it without reference to the original. They can recall it in their mind accurately and can use it in meditation. When the pupil is fully intimate with their mandala, they give it back to their teacher to show that they are ready to learn.

The mandala represents what the teacher wants to instruct his pupil in. The whole mandala represents human experience, the circle represents eternity, and the square inside the circle the deity that the teacher wants to induct the pupil into. Typically, there are four gates into the deity, one on each side of the square.

Meditation. The practice of concentrated focus upon a sound, object, visualisation, the breath in order to increase awareness of the present moment. Meditation reduces stress, promotes relaxation and enhances personal and spiritual growth.

Power of Three. The combined powers of three entities. Such a combination not only increases their power by three, but by a much greater exponent. Examples are the Holy Trinity (Father, Son and Holy Spirit), and body, mind and soul.

Reiki. A therapy often described as palm or hands-on-body healing. The reiki master places hands lightly on or over the person's body to facilitate the healing process. Reiki combines the Japanese and Chinese words of 'rei' meaning spiritual or supernatural and 'ki' which means vital energy. The reiki master channels this vital energy to support the body's natural ability to heal.

Sacred Geometry. Geometric shapes have been recognised as representing something nonphysical for many thousands of years. Sacred Geometry utilises the inherent power of the shape or number. It is a common global heritage seen in the cultures of the Incas, Native American Indians, tribes of Africa, Egyptians, Romans, Asian Indians and Australian Aborigines. Sacred Geometry is seen in sacred rites and structures made by peoples to represent the celestial on Earth, which links Earth to the heavens.

Soul Art. Painting of geometric shapes to aid relaxation and reflection. Geometric shapes are a fundamental building block of life. Soul Art is a technique to aid identifying members of your family and friends with whom you have shared many lives. It is a personal development tool for a deeper understanding of yourself and your external family and the lessons you are learning over many millennia.

Resources

Current Life Review Chart

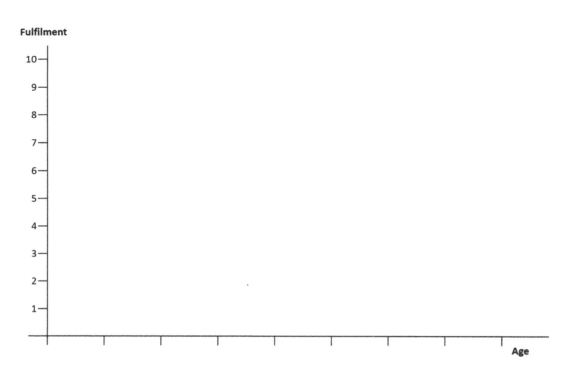

Life Observation Chart

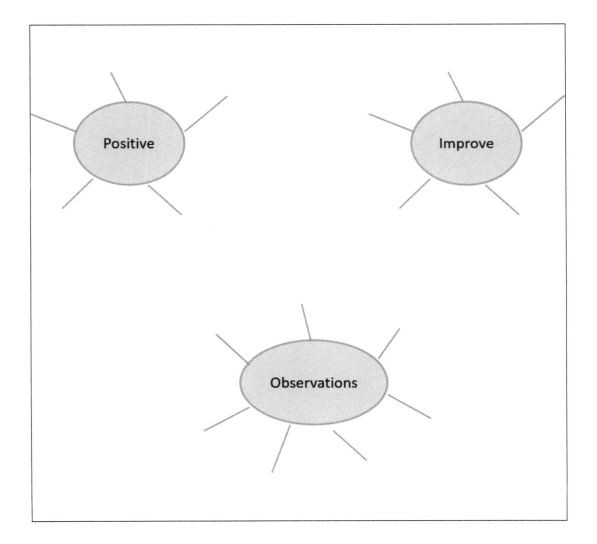

Family Information Table: Your Life Lessons and Special Relationships

Note: Try to complete columns 1–3. If you are unsure of the life lesson but know you are linked, see if there is a special relationship.

Name of key person in your life (a soul family member)	Your Life Lesson the key person is helping you with	Life Lesson you are helping the key person with	Special Relationship between you if a Life Lesson cannot be identified

Family Information Table: Family Member Life Lessons and Special Relationships

Note: Try to complete columns 1–3. If you are unsure of the life lesson but know two family members are linked, see if there is a special relationship.

Name of key person in your life (a soul family member)	Name of key person(s) in your life with a relationship with the column 1 person	Life Lesson being learnt	Special Relationship between these people if a Life Lesson cannot be identified

Thought Diary

Date	Thought/Dream/Insight	Follow-up Action

Colour Counters

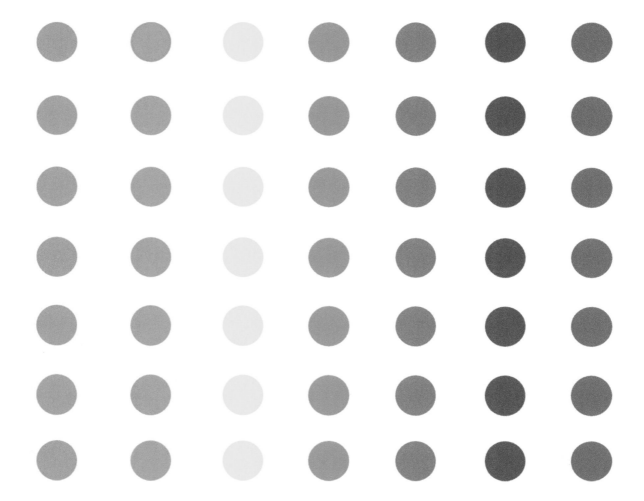

Chakra Symbol Counters

Sahasrara: The Crown Chakra

Sahasrara: The Crown Chakra

Sahasrara: The Crown Chakra

Sahasrara: The Crown Chakra

Ajna: The Brow Chakra

Ajna: The Brow Chakra

Ajna: The Brow Chakra

Ajna: The Brow Chakra

Vishuddha: The Throat Chakra

Vishuddha: The Throat Chakra

Vishuddha: The Throat Chakra

Vishuddha: The Throat Chakra

Anahata: The Heart Chakra

Anahata: The Heart Chakra

Anahata: The Heart Chakra

Anahata: The Heart Chakra

Manipura: The Solar Plexus Chakra

Manipura: The Solar Plexus Chakra

Manipura: The Solar Plexus Chakra

Manipura: The Solar Plexus Chakra

Swadhisthana: The Sacral Chakra

Swadhisthana: The Sacral Chakra

Swadhisthana: The Sacral Chakra

Swadhisthana: The Sacral Chakra

Muladhara: The Base Chakra

Muladhara: The Base Chakra

Muladhara: The Base Chakra

Muladhara: The Base Chakra

Foundation Template

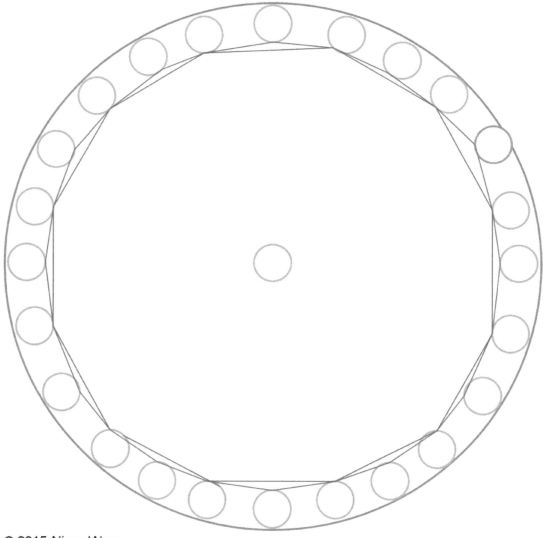

Daffodil Template

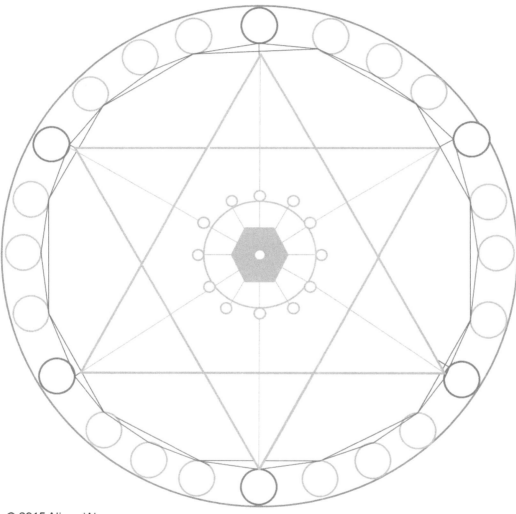

Celtic Cross Template

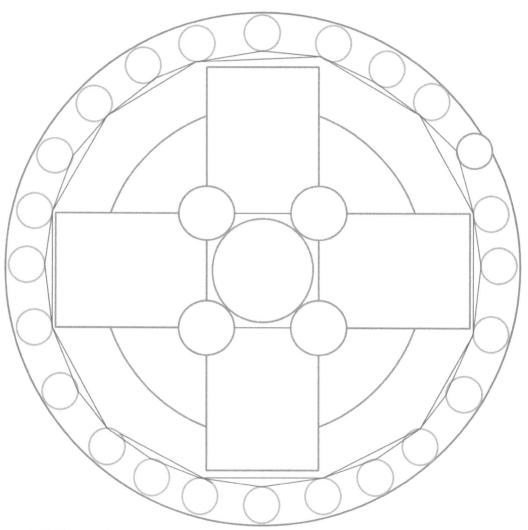

Tibetan Buddhism Template

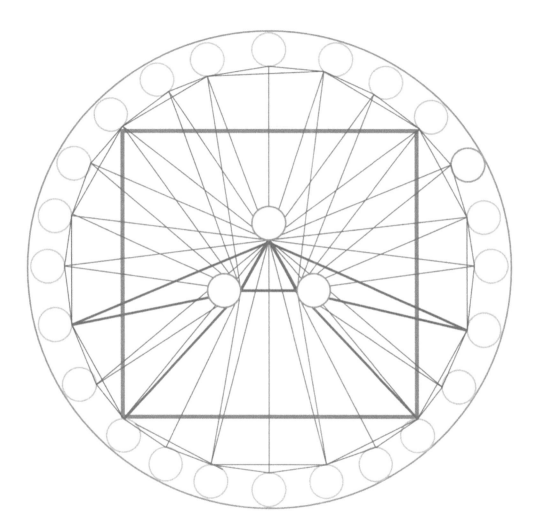

Hexagram Template

Interlocking Circles Template

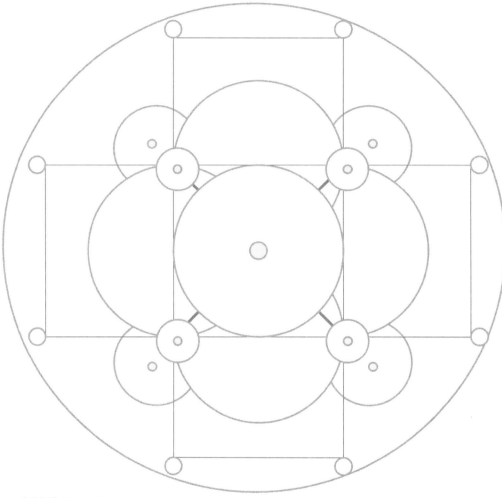

Balance and Symmetry Template

Spiral Template

Index